The Hardest Questions Aren't on the Test

The Hardest Questions Aren't on the Test

Lessons from an
Innovative Urban School

Linda F. Nathan

BEACON PRESS
Boston

Beacon Press
25 Beacon Street
Boston, Massachusetts 02108-2892
www.beacon.org

Beacon Press books
are published under the auspices of
the Unitarian Universalist Association of Congregations.

13 12 11 10   8 7 6 5 4 3 2 1

This book is printed on acid-free paper that meets the uncoated paper
ANSI/NISO specifications for permanence as revised in 1992.

Library of Congress Cataloging-in-Publication Data
Nathan, Linda F.
  The hardest questions aren't on the test : lessons from an innovative urban
school / Linda F. Nathan.
     p. cm.
  Includes bibliographical references.
  ISBN 978-0-8070-0615-3 (paperback: alk. paper) 1. School improvement
programs—Massachusetts—Boston—Case studies. 2. Education, Urban—
Massachusetts—Boston—Case studies. 3. High schools—Massachusetts—
Boston—Case studies. I. Title.
  LB2822.83.M4N38 2009
  371.2´070974461—dc22   2009010397

Text design and composition by M. F. Rutherglen
at Wilsted & Taylor Publishing Services

This is a true account except that in many cases I have used
composites and pseudonyms to protect privacy.

Dedicated to Vito Perrone, my friend and mentor,
and my three children, Samuel, Benjamin, and Abigail,
the next generation of teachers

Contents

Introduction

It was one of those typical New England days in March with the snow pelting down but not really collecting much on the streets. The wind was blowing hard, making it seem much colder. I kept glancing at the television, hoping that someone with sense would cancel school in Boston. Other schools in the surrounding cities and towns were canceled, but not us. I was sure that some teachers wouldn't be able to make it in, but kids would come, and that would make for a chaotic day trying to figure out classroom coverage. Maybe the weather would be a blessing, since the theater department was behind in its rehearsal schedule, and if some academic classes were canceled, then the theater faculty could pull kids earlier in the day for rehearsal. I looked at my agenda: a school visit day! A large group from a comprehensive high school in a neighboring suburban community was scheduled to arrive. I couldn't remember what questions they were interested in pursuing, but if their school was canceled, I hoped that they wouldn't come. I rushed out to my car to scrape the snow and ice off and slowly made my way into school, still hoping against hope that I'd hear a cancellation on the radio.

As I arrived at school, Buddy, our head custodian, was clearing the sidewalks with a snowblower. He shook his head at me as if to say, "Who didn't have the sense to cancel school today?" I ruefully smiled back with the same feeling of exasperation. Just then the serviceman delivering coffee and bagels for our new visitors pulled in. Corey Evans, our Center for Arts in Education director, was setting up the VCR and the chairs in the assembly hall, preparing for whoever came, just in case. Students began trooping in. Their voices rang out as they greeted one another, hugged and kissed, and even chased each other down the hallways as if they had been separated for weeks instead of just a night. They slipped and slid on their ways to the cafeteria for breakfast or to their lockers to get ready for first period, wet snow dripping off coats and boots leaving puddles everywhere. Mike, Buddy's assistant custodian, was patiently mopping the lobby area, trying to keep the floors from getting so slick that students would hurt themselves. "Watch out now. Slow down a bit," he reminded students who were too exuberant with their good morning wishes.

As I anticipated today's visitors, I thought back to a group that had come last month, from a school labeled "underperforming" by the Department of Education. They had been told that they must decide within four weeks either to design a new school and possibly convert to some kind of pilot status or face a state takeover. They were to "learn the lessons of Boston Arts Academy." Their urban school, which for decades had had poor student achievement, was now miraculously meant to turn around after visiting us and seeing the "light." I had thought at the time that this was a "setup," a recipe for disaster. How could one visit ever be an antidote to years of underperformance? And what teacher or principal likes to be told, "Here's what you *should* be doing..."

The Boston Arts Academy's mission is to be a "laboratory and a beacon for artistic and academic innovation," and as such we regularly have teachers and educational leaders coming to learn about our curriculum, programs, and structures. We are an eleven-year-old pilot school that operates within the Boston Public School district, but we have considerable freedom to create our own curriculum. We also have the ability (unlike most public or charter schools) to select our students through an audition process. We do not look at prospective students' academic records (we call this an academic-blind application process), but we do screen them for passion and commitment to pursuing their chosen art form (music, dance, theater, or visual arts) seriously. Approximately 400 students audition each year for about 140 seats. We can accept only students who live in the city of Boston.

Our school is small (420), and our diversity mirrors that of our district, Boston Public Schools (our students are 48 percent African American, 30 percent Latino, 17 percent white, 3 percent Asian, and less than 3 percent Native American and other). In terms of socio-economics, BAA has approximately 60 percent of its students on free or reduced lunch; the district is at 71 percent: we have definitely attracted more middle-class students to our school. In terms of special education, 13 percent of our students have identified special needs, compared to a district rate of 20 percent. We also have a small number of students identified as English language learners (under 6 percent), whereas the district has a larger number (18 percent) since many schools have what is now called Sheltered English Language programs, formerly known as bilingual education. Presently, we do not have a bilingual program, though we have a deaf education program. We are very lucky to have a diverse faculty as well. Of our forty-five teachers, 50 percent are teachers of color. The percentage of teachers of color in Massachusetts is just under 10 percent. Over half of our teachers are first generation to attend college themselves; 50 percent speak a language other than English; and 95 percent have advanced degrees, some more than one. We have an active gay, lesbian, bisexual, and questioning community among our students, which is supported by gay and straight staff members. We are proud that 95 percent of our students go on to college, in striking contrast with the average within Boston Public Schools, which is under 50 percent. Our school is housed in an adequate, but by no means luxurious, building in the Fenway area of Boston, which we share with another pilot school, Fenway High School. Because our school is both different from "typical" public high schools and successful by measures that matter to policy makers locally and nationally, we host lots of visitors each year, including teams of teachers and leaders from schools interested in implementing changes.

I try hard not to present myself and the staff of BAA as having all the answers, but rather as willing to ask those tough questions. Sometimes I call this "sharing our warts and wounds," which is another way of saying we try not to whitewash our struggles. But no matter how self-consciously and even humbly we prepare ourselves, I thought, the visitors who have been forced to come are unlikely to learn much from us. To my surprise, though, a group of visitors we had come by the school last month had been impressed listening to our students, very much like their own, describe their struggles and triumphs in the classroom. One student talked about being homeless and how BAA's Student Support team found her housing and part-time employment so she could be more financially independent while continuing at school. She had passed all but one of her classes that semester. The visitors had nodded sadly at her story. Each one of them knew students in similar or worse situations.

A group of BAA's native Spanish speakers talked about a project in Spanish class: to write an original story and then go to the local bilingual school to read those stories aloud to younger bilingual students. Their teacher explained that for many of her students, who previously had not been doing very well in school, completing a project in their home language allowed them to see how their academic work connected to their lives and to their communities. "My students loved feeling so important to those second-graders! Some were even asked for their autograph like they were published authors. And every single one of my students finished on time, and did the assignment very well." The visitors' eyes lit up. "Yes, this is an activity that we could do, too," they seemed to say.

But as BAA teachers and students talked about whole-school initiatives—such as when we all visit colleges, or school-wide community days or assemblies, or weekly professional development seminars, or the integration of arts and academics, or our portfolio assessment system, or the role of parent and student leadership, or even our advisory system—the visitors were quiet, almost aloof. Those endeavors, I thought, seemed much too overwhelming. Individual classroom efforts were possible, but not a whole-school enterprise in which everyone participated.

Enough thinking about last month's visit, I had to get ready for today's, if, indeed, it was going to happen at all.

I could feel that the day would be bedlam, since I already knew that four teachers couldn't get in because of the storm. I was talking through first period logistics with Ramiro and Marc, both science teachers, and asked if one of them would cover for Alex, who was stuck in traffic. I explained that the substitute teacher had just called to say that he wouldn't be able to make it in either. Seth, a theater teacher, came in at that point with a large group of students who had just gotten off the 51 bus. "I'm glad to see you," I told him. "No one else from your department is in. I've asked all the freshmen and sophomore theater majors to wait in the café. I was just trying to figure out if I was going to teach acting to forty kids!"

"Not a problem. I can take them all for the first hour, and then I think Ms. TC will get here and we can split up. I'll bring them upstairs now!"

Just as I was trying to figure out where to send upper-class students who had humanities and no teacher, I saw a number of unfamiliar faces: our visitors. Oh boy. The teachers stuck out not just because they were strangers to me, but also because they were all white. Many of them had that slightly awkward, even a bit frightened air that characterizes middle-class white people suddenly surrounded by crowds of loud, mostly black kids. I didn't fault them for it.

I introduced myself as I ushered the group out of the noisy and crowded lobby into the assembly hall, where they struggled out of their snowy coats and drifted or rushed to the coffee and bagels. Teachers everywhere in the world, I find, are happy and a bit surprised to be treated with respect and hospitality. At conventions, educators are the ones noticing with excitement that the meeting rooms have comfortable chairs and pitchers of ice water. "Wow, what a treat!" they think, and sometimes say. Would members of any other profession react like this? I took a second to address the visitors: "Get yourselves settled and I'll be right back with you. I just have to figure out how we are covering a few classrooms. We're glad you're here. I didn't think you'd make it. I thought I heard on the news that your schools had been canceled." I hoped I didn't sound as scattered as I felt.

Back out in the hall, I spied Shawn from the junior humanities class. "Shawn, can you take Ms. Diaz's class upstairs and get started? Do you know what you are doing today?"

"We're working in groups reading each other's ten-page essays. Not everyone's pairs are here, but I'm sure we can figure something out." With that, he beckoned to his classmates and they trooped off. Thank goodness for responsible students, I thought. We work hard at BAA to inculcate and reward this kind of behavior, and it surely pays off.

"Are we going to get an extension on the paper?" Jessica asked me. "It's not really fair that we have to present tomorrow if our group members aren't all here."

"Let's wait till Ms. Diaz arrives and then she can have that conversation with you."

"I just think you should say that we won't have our grade lowered or anything. You know how the teachers can be and they might say we had this deadline no matter what and I don't think that'd be fair."

"I wouldn't worry just now, Jessica." I tried to make myself sound patient though I knew Jessica was on thin ice in terms of whether she was passing, and I suspected she was using the snowstorm as a way to give herself more time to finish the assignment. "You should probably catch up with your class now." She sidled off, still muttering to herself about the fact that it wasn't fair because of the weather. Ah, I thought. Just when I was feeling a bit smug after talking to Shawn, Jessica reminded me that BAA kids can be just as annoying and whiny as high school kids everywhere.

I returned to the visitors waiting in the assembly hall. One of the members of the group, a tall man with graying temples and sparkling eyes, introduced himself as the leader for the visit.

"It took us six months to get permission to come for this visit. It would have taken more than a little snow to stop us from coming. I hope it's okay, but I think there will be more than twelve of us now." Even in the midst of my swirling thoughts, his comment and enthusiasm brought me back to a sense of gratitude and pride. Here were all these teachers, working hard to get here, and being excited about seeing our school. I felt myself relax and focus.

"Of course it's okay. We are excited that so many of you made the effort to come." After getting everyone settled with their coffee, Corey and I began the formal school visit. Some of our student ambassadors had joined us, and more begged to be part of the morning school tour. "Our teachers are out and there's no substitute. We'll be of more use here!" Corey and I decided that we could, in fact, pair up visitors with students in groups of one or two and give them a more intimate orientation to the school.

The visitors were from a suburban community just outside Boston. They came from a school that was considered one of the best in the state in terms of course offerings, college admissions, and passing rates on the MCAS (Massachusetts Comprehensive Assessment System) test. Many families moved to this community because of the school system. But the teachers expressed a great deal of disgruntlement. The lead teacher, Gary, explained: "We want to break down into small learning communities. It is just too much to get to know two thousand students. If we are in smaller schools, then students will learn better; they'll care more about school; they'll care more about each other. Right now it's pretty cutthroat. Getting good grades is all that counts for most kids. They don't care who they step over to get them—including us. I've been here for twenty-seven years and I've seen it all, let me tell you!"

Others echoed this sentiment. "We've held so many community meetings with parents and school meetings with students, and even though there is tremendous resistance to breaking up the school—everyone's afraid that it will destroy our music program, or our AP offerings, you name it—we've gotten to a place where folks are willing to listen to a plan if we can provide a coherent one," said one.

Another one of the teachers, Shelly, a small woman with heavy jewelry and coifed blond hair, interjected, "To be fair so that you understand the complexity of it all: there's been a lot of controversy over the idea of small learning communities. It's not just that parents and others are afraid of what we'll lose, but also they don't really see how 'small' is an answer. They just aren't convinced that small makes a difference in high school. And to be quite honest, neither are some of us. I went to a big high school and it was just fine."

To me, this teacher had hit on the essence of what makes changing schools so difficult. Most teachers became teachers because they did well in school. The system worked for them: it worked "just fine." How can teachers truly grapple with different approaches than those they experienced as a student? I've found as I listen to teachers describe their childhood schools that often they don't take into account that they were the successful students—what about the others?

In many comprehensive high schools there is the honors track, the college prep track, the standard track, the vocational track, and sometimes even more tracks. Often only the students in the honors track take Advanced Placement (AP) courses. Students in the college track quickly learn that it is really the students in the honors track who get the most counseling about what courses are required to enter a competitive college. Teachers, who were successful students in their youth and generally placed in the honors track, usually describe the tracking of their former high schools with little critique. They acknowledge that there were few students of color in the AP or honors tracks, but they quickly add that everyone mixed in music and sports. Often they go so far as to say that their high school was really great and quite diverse. Another one of the visitors, a middle-aged man with thinning hair and a ponytail, interrupted my silent thoughts about how powerful phrases such as "just fine" are in fact colored by one's own background and experiences.

"Still, we've decided that block scheduling is the answer." He spoke with his hands, gesticulating for emphasis. "If we can just have students for longer periods of time," he opened his hands widely, "then things will improve. That part of the plan has been approved, but we need to do more to convince folks about small learning communities."

I wondered about the certainty with which this teacher approached block scheduling as *the* answer. Could these teachers push themselves to ask about small learning communities with the same certainty? Again and again, I'm struck by how difficult it is for us to ask the hard questions in schools.

I asked, "So what are the questions you are coming with today?"

Various teachers responded that they wanted to learn more about the successes and challenges of scheduling in longer blocks of time, instead of the typical fifty-minute class periods. They also said they had heard that we were a full-inclusion high school and they wanted to know about integrating special-needs students into the regular classes. "We can't give up AP, but we sure need to do a better job with the students who struggle the most academically, and who are often our special education students," said one teacher.

"And really, my main question is about how to introduce small learning communities to our school. I know it's a political issue, too, within our larger community, but I'd like to have the chance to talk about that," said another.

I felt confident that over the course of the day our visitors would have the opportunity to pursue the questions they had brought with them. But beyond finding answers, I hoped that they would notice the many conflicts and choices that are inherent in the way we make decisions at BAA. And most important, I hoped they would realize that questions are an essential part of our process. I believe that it was, and continues to be, the ability and courage to ask and to pursue complex and often uncomfortable questions that charts our course. It is those very questions that keep us focused on our students and their needs.

Our student ambassadors jumped up, ready to show off their school, and we set off.

As we walked up the stairs to the third floor, Rajon stopped us on the landing. He introduced himself and shook everyone's hand in the group like the perfect gentleman that he is. Rajon dresses impeccably, not in overly fancy clothes, but always neat and with pressed pants and a tie. Once I asked him why he wore a tie, since we have nothing even close to a school uniform. "For me wearing a tie means that I am taking something seriously. I take school seriously. I think sometimes you act the part you look like." Looking at him I was struck by how closely he matches the stereotype of a prep school student—close-cropped hair, button-down shirt, tie, pressed pants. Only the sneakers give him away. He speaks with clear diction and when he smiles the whole world wants to grin along with him. His looks are infectious that way, and his voice, too, has a resonance that makes you want to follow any point he makes. He spoke warmly to our visitors, who looked impressed and a bit amazed. "I'm a music major here. Vocalist. I'm also leading a new men's chorus we've developed, a way to give young men here more responsibility, and to let them compose and sing about their issues, especially as young men of color. Too many of us are dropping out or in prison. We gotta change that. I'm a senior but I'll graduate next January. I hope you can come to our Spring Concert. It's going to be wonderful." And with that, he headed down the stairs to his class.

I turned to one of the teachers and said, "It's amazing how far he's come. Just looking at the way he dresses now takes me aback. He was out of control when he came. Fighting with everyone. He had already been kicked out of two high schools. But he has a voice like an angel and we thought we could work with him. He's got some serious learning disabilities and won't get a high school diploma—just a certificate of attendance—because he can't pass the MCAS. He's taken it five times. He testified last year at the State House. I carry his testimony around with me." I unfolded a crumpled piece of paper and smoothed it out so that the teacher next to me could read it.

I have decided that there are more important things to focus on, like learning about the world in Humanities and learning technique in Music, instead of being pulled out to keep testing.

It is not fair that the MCAS messes with people's future and can stop them from graduating.

Some students feel like failures and might drop out of school. Not me. I will get my certificate of attendance next June.

MCAS only tests some of the skills that are important to have when you graduate from high school.

Coming from a rough neighborhood, school is a place to learn:

>*to be respected*

>*to be a better person*

>*to deal with different kinds of people*

>*to feel good about myself.*

The MCAS only causes me and other people to loose [sic] confidence.

I don't want my younger brother and sister to go through this.

If I had my wish, I wouldn't want anymore [sic] young achievers to be stopped from graduating by not passing the MCAS. The MCAS does not show anything these young people know.

I hope all the lawmakers of Massachusetts will consider getting rid of the MCAS.

All that it does is hurt kids. Thank you.

Rajon had signed the paper. The teacher looked at it and asked if she could pass it to her colleagues. Teachers nodded as they read his words. The last teacher returned it to me and I carefully tucked it away. "That's really sad," she said. "He's such a lovely young man. We are lucky that at our school we don't have this issue, really. All our kids pass the MCAS. Usually on the first take. But it sure has curtailed what we teach—even the way we teach. We have to make sure we teach to the test. Our parents wouldn't stand for their kids not passing."

I told the group that although Rajon was an extreme case, we had many students who needed to take the MCAS more than once. "There are so many other ways to measure student achievement, beyond a fill-in-the-blank test. I want to open up the whole discussion about assessment so that we really grapple with what it means for a student to understand something well. I understand the need for these kinds of easy-to-score tests that will give us quick information about students and schools, but I am so saddened by what it does to our students. Why isn't it valid for Rajon to show his learning through a series of portfolios? I would be somewhat okay if MCAS was just one indicator of how a student was doing, not a high-stakes test that determines graduation. I honestly don't know how it helps Rajon that he won't get a diploma, just a certificate of attendance." I was getting out of breath and talking faster as I cruised along, describing one of my biggest educational frustrations. I caught myself and stopped. Oh yeah. I wasn't here to convince them of anything, right? In the pause, the visitors nodded sympathetically.

"It must be hard for you. Our kids really have so many more resources. It's really about how much you read before you are, let's say, eight or nine, isn't it?" one of the teachers suggested.

"Right," I responded, "and too many of our students come from families where having books in the home, going to the library, just having a set place and time to do homework doesn't happen. That's not an excuse. It's just the reality for too many of our kids."

The teacher nodded again.

I wanted more than a sympathetic nod. I wanted everyone to remember that knowledge and achievement cannot be determined by one cookie-cutter method alone. Rajon can write—he wrote this testimony—and he obviously can think. He's a wonderful artist, too. Yet the current rules that determine school success don't value or reward his talents. Of course students need to know content, but I am more interested in how they articulate questions and pose problems and solutions than I am in whether they know all of world civilization for a state test. It seems to me that this is the essential struggle between me and those who advocate for high-stakes tests that are easy and quick to score and judge. Spokesmen for the tests often say, "We need to know what kids know—that's the point of school." I agree that that is *part* of the point of school. But efficient scoring of tests does not make a better educational system, does it? What if we constructed a system with multiple ways of demonstrating what students know and can do? If Rajon had the opportunity to design his own portfolio system with his teachers, I think the public would see that he did know "stuff." Sometimes I think that I could spend a lifetime trying to convince policy makers that demonstrating student learning need not just be through bubble sheets—and I might not succeed.

With an effort, I stopped my internal monologue about testing as I brought the visitors into a theater classroom where students were working on scenes from August Wilson's *Fences*. Suddenly, one of the students flew out the door, banging it behind her in anger. The teacher, Ms. Yarborough, quietly walked out behind her, instructing the other students to continue with their work. The door remained open and we overheard their conversation. "What happened in there, Pamela?" the teacher asked firmly.

"I'm just sick of everything having to do with race here. I hate this play and when you make us do this kind of stuff then all we talk about is how white people are bad. It's not my fault about slavery. It's not my fault that I'm white."

Ms. Yarborough quietly responded. "This doesn't have to do with *you* being white. You are playing a scene. You are learning to be an actor, to think like the character you are playing. What does Rose care about? What does she love? What makes her angry?"

"I know. I know and I knew you'd say that. But why do we always have to do plays like this? I'm just sick of it."

"We do lots of different plays here, but this term we are working on this play. Now, I need you to go back in that room and get that scene ready to be performed for the class. This play does bring up a lot of stuff, whether we like that stuff or not. Race is always right in front of us. Right under the surface. Right on our skin—"

"I knew you'd say that, too," Pamela interrupted her. "That's what I'm saying. I don't *want* to always talk about race. I just want us to be friends. Just forget it. I'm going back." With that, she stomped back in the room as angrily as she had left.

I ushered our visitors out of the classroom into the hallway where the interchange between Pamela and Ms. Yarborough had just occurred. I shut the door to the classroom on the students who were continuing to rehearse their scenes; no one had stopped working while Ms. Yarborough was out of the room. Most of the visitors had looks of shock and disapproval on their faces. "I'm not sure our teachers of color could ever talk to our white students like that, not that I've ever even seen a student act like that," one of them commented. "We have so few students of color anyway at our school. I don't think those issues even *exist* on our campus."

I didn't say anything then. But I was sure "those issues" did exist on her campus. Race issues are everywhere, whether we see them or not. I bristled inside but stopped myself from launching into a speech about how I believe that learning to talk about race is central to achievement for all students. I forced myself to remember that comments like these can be someone's way of asking a hard question. No more diatribes from me!

"Well," another teacher began, "even if those issues *are* on our campus, I felt uncomfortable seeing such an intense teacher-student conversation in the hallway. It felt like that student's privacy was being violated. I have to ask myself, 'Is this really appropriate for school?'"

Again, I stopped myself from giving a passionate retort. Quietly, I responded, "Well, to me, school has to be a place where discussion and confrontation of the '-isms' in our society—about race, class, gender, language, sexual orientation, and the list can go on—all are part of our ongoing daily work. If not, I often ask myself, 'What is the point of all this?'" To myself I thought, Don't we have a responsibility to provide forums and places where students and teachers interact in authentic ways across differences? I looked up at my visitors' faces— some had blank looks. I wasn't sure how they were taking all this.

Amanda, one of the student ambassadors who had been part of the tour, asked if she could add some of her comments. "First of all, it isn't easy to talk about differences. We just want to be able to be kids and ignore all that. I came from a suburban school system, very much like yours. BAA was a real culture shock for me in lots of ways.

"I was used to being in the honors track and I was getting ready for all AP classes, but when I came here as a sophomore I learned that there was no AP, just dual enrollment, which means we could take classes at some of the colleges around here. I also learned that there was no separate honors track, only what we call 'open honors,' which means you do extra work within the class. I kind of resent that I have to be motivated myself to do the extra work. Sometimes I feel like I'm slowed down by some of my classmates, at least in my academic classes."

"We couldn't get away with that," one of the visitors said immediately. "Our parents would freak out. So would the kids. How would they get into Harvard? I can hear the objections now."

Another teacher disagreed. "I don't know. I think we've never raised that question. I think it would be a fascinating topic for discussion."

"More like a bloodbath," the other teacher countered.

I interrupted. "I like to tell people that this school is ten years old and has had eleven different schedules. We keep trying to figure out ways to give more support to those students who need it and more enrichment to students like Amanda. Balancing both ends of the spectrum of students' skills has been a central question for us since we opened our doors. We don't have it right yet."

"To me, that sounds too chaotic," said the teacher who felt that tracking was here to stay. "It just stretches a teacher too much. Who can meet all those needs in the same classroom?"

"But," I asked, "what if you were transparent about what you were trying to do and the difficulties involved? Then, wouldn't the community perhaps be more tolerant?"

The teacher winced as I spoke. "That's a loaded word for us: 'transparent,'" he told me. "I'm not sure our community would tolerate really knowing the reasons behind things. I always feel that our community—you know, parents and others who graduated from the school—wants school to be just the way they knew it." The visitors nodded in agreement.

I thought about the truth in these words. It is what makes school-reform work so difficult. Everyone is an expert about schools because most everyone has been to school. If I've learned one thing in the past thirty years of my own work to change schools, it is that reform is essentially political and that you must know your community's context before plunging in. I would never have even thought about "transparent" as a touchy word. This small fact helped me envision the kind of community the visiting teachers were working in. Everyone faces different problems, I thought. Privilege and wealth don't always make things easier for educators.

When I think about my work at school, I know my colleagues and I are undertaking a fragile dance with the potential for many missteps. I also know that success is possible when I, in close collaboration with my colleagues, am able to clearly articulate those essential questions that frame our community's needs.

I am continually reminded of something Vito Perrone—my friend and mentor, and author of one my favorite books, *A Letter to Teachers*—said to me back in the early 1980s. He was listening to me argue with a group of my teachers about homework. We were going back and forth about what to do about the fact that students didn't do their homework on a regular basis. We were discussing all sorts of draconian ways to punish them and grade them lower so that they would be motivated to do homework. Quietly, Vito asked, "Why do you give homework?" We were stunned, and the discussion stopped momentarily. The obvious answer, "Because we always have," clearly wasn't good enough. That simple question led us down a path where we gave ourselves permission to ask those seemingly straightforward, but in fact very complicated, "why" questions.

I've tried to bring that same philosophy to BAA. It's not really about answers or solutions, although we all want practices that work better, but it *is* about asking questions. Over the years, with a great deal of hard work from everyone involved, we have gotten better at expressing our successes and failures, and describing our learning process. As I talked with the visiting team after their observations, I mentioned this idea.

"Still, at the end of the day," a teacher responded, "for us it's about the number of students admitted to competitive four-year colleges. Everything else is just fluff. I don't know how you change that equation."

"I'm not sure I know the exact answer, but I know that the conversation about achievement has to be about more than scores on standardized tests. Everywhere in this country schools are talking about 'closing the achievement gap,' or 'equity and access,' but what do those phrases really mean? How do we apply them to daily school life with all constituents—" I stopped myself suddenly. "Oh dear, I've gotten on my soapbox. But really I'm trying to say that everything that happens at our school begins with the framing questions that we ask. That's what makes it so exciting."

As the visitors packed up their things and said good-bye, I looked at their faces and body language. Many of them had that glazed-over look that comes with too much information. Others were thoughtful, withdrawn into themselves. They were starting to mull over what they had seen, I thought. In the early days of visitors coming to my school, I would have felt let down if the faces had not registered awe and admiration, if the teachers hadn't seemed inspired. I wanted them to cheer us on, to affirm my own sense of how well we were doing. Now though, I was happy to see this different reaction. The teachers, I suspected, were leaving our school thinking about *their* school. Maybe they were gearing up for arguments. Hopefully, they were forming more questions.

The stories I offer in this book are examples of how my colleagues and I have grappled with a series of questions. I believe that the questions we as school leaders and teachers ask can set in motion an entire course of action, driving everything that goes on in our school: from scheduling and course offerings, to disciplinary and grading policies, to our relationships with students and with one another.

Each day I meet another teacher or school leader who has the courage and desire to ask questions that may go against the norm or standard. Teachers and principals know that we cannot afford to let yet another generation of young people pass through our hallways and classrooms and leave feeling disengaged and angry. Teachers and principals can find a way, with their colleagues, and within their schools, larger communities, teacher organizations, unions, and other professional organizations, to pose questions for themselves and their own schools. I ask myself, as I think all educators should ask themselves: What does your school stand for? How do you make curriculum relevant? What roles do teachers, leaders, and students play in helping to shape the school? What are the questions we are avoiding asking? What are the questions *behind* the problems we are facing?

Schools may use different means than those I have developed at BAA to achieve similar ends—in fact, they must. Every school is unique, and every solution is, too. Perhaps a school might aim to engage students primarily through science and technology instead of the arts. Or perhaps one school's core values place more emphasis on individual efforts than on group interactions. Nevertheless, as teachers and administrators thoughtfully take the time *to know and live what their school is about,* they are determining a new course of action for their school, and I believe that they are also ensuring better outcomes for their students.

More than ever we, as educators, must find ways to invent new possibilities for urban high schools—in fact, for all high schools. I don't believe our schools are working as they could be. It's not up to principals and school leaders to make the changes, but it *is* up to us to continue asking the hardest questions. I offer my journey through the thorny territory into which these questions inevitably lead, not as a guide or a prescription, but as a picture of the territory itself. I want to let you know that someone who has been on this journey for a long time still finds it a joyous and enormously important one.

The Hardest Questions Aren't on the Test

Part I

Structuring a School

1. What Does This School *Really* Stand For?

How to move from endless initiatives to a unifying framework?

My first year of teaching I worked for a school that had a guiding philosophy called "Focus on Reading." Posters hung in hallways and in every classroom, store-bought as well as student illustrated, encouraging everyone to read. *Reading Is Fundamental! Reading Is Fun!* Some featured celebrities and sports heroes holding favorite childhood books. Others depicted cartoon characters engrossed in reading: *Garfield loves to read!*

At the opening-day meeting, our principal stood onstage and exhorted the entire faculty—math, science, and music teachers included—to make reading our focus. "Each and every one of you needs to make time in your lessons to make sure your students are reading," he said. "There is no reason why our scores are some of the lowest in the district. We're going to change that. We're going to make sure that all of our students pass the citywide reading test this spring. Let's move to the top of this list." The curriculum coordinator followed, explaining that she would make individual appointments with each of us to see how we "did reading" in our content areas and how she could help us do more and better. The meeting had a bit of a pep-rally feeling to it and I felt swept up in the excitement. But I noticed many veteran faculty shuffling papers, glancing at newspapers, and yawning indiscreetly. "What is it this year?" their body language seemed to say. "No reason to get worked up. We'll wait out this new initiative, just like all the others."

Their cynicism wasn't entirely without cause, as I was soon to discover. Come spring, reading exams taken and results in, the faculty assembled again, this time with coffee and doughnuts waiting for us in the assembly hall, and the principal and his administrative team in a celebratory mood. I'd thrown myself into the new initiative and was excited to hear the results.

"We've moved to the top third of the list!" the principal announced with a broad smile, waving his data sheets. "We're no longer a failure in the district. I am so proud that all of you could keep such a sustained focus on reading. Clearly our students have benefited from your efforts."

Our students—my students!—had done well on the test. I was elated that all of our hard work had paid off. But I was also left with a nagging, sinking feeling. When it came right down to it, what did these positive test scores actually measure? While I felt confident that my students had grown as readers, I doubted that these scores were evidence that they were better thinkers and learners in any fundamental or holistic way. Nor was I sure my students had actually learned to transfer the material from one format to another. I was passionate about how my students were developing, but they—and I and my school as well—were being measured and ranked by their performance on *one* standardized reading test. I worried aloud to some of my colleagues whether our students would do as well if they were given a different kind of reading test, a test that asked them to analyze, or to predict, or to think critically, as opposed to answering questions that required literal comprehension.

"Just wait," a colleague told me glumly. "This too shall pass."

He was right. When we assembled in the fall, the principal announced that this year's focus would be math. "Of course, don't give up your terrific work on reading, but the district has purchased brand-new textbooks and is implementing a new math program at all grade levels." I wanted to be happy; I was a math teacher, after all. But it seemed ludicrous that we were on to something else. We'd just gotten started and I wanted more time to flesh out the reading initiative and make it my own. I caught my colleague's eye as he mouthed the words, "I told you so."

Don't get me wrong—there's nothing wrong with a new initiative. New initiatives can bring needed energy, focus, training, and technical skills to a faculty. And often they are based on sound educational thinking. But while "sloganeering" each year about a different curricular area might provide focus and boost scores for the short term, it doesn't necessarily create a community where everyone—teachers, students, administrators, and parents—feels a sense of ownership in developing students' intellectual potential. Yes, the principal successfully met the district mandates: raise reading scores and improve math scores.

While vital goals, these are much too limited and lead to a limited set of questions with limited answers. Ultimately, these kinds of slogans, masked as goals, don't take into account a broad approach to teaching and learning that will raise student achievement for the long haul. These initiatives are short-term "fixes" that meet the current mandates, even successfully, but rarely provide a school community the kind of power that a unifying philosophy might. It is not wrong to raise test scores, but without an expanded set of questions about what we are about as a school community, test scores will just rise and fall with whatever criteria the current test agenda has put forth. None of the initiatives will have led to lasting fundamental changes in teaching and learning in a school. It would have been better to have found a way to make our reading or math initiatives the basis of more complicated discussions about teaching and learning, about the ways in which we were developing a vibrant school community, and about the ways we did or did not work as a faculty. But that didn't happen.

TURNING AWAY FROM THE ENDLESS INITIATIVES; TURNING TOWARD ASKING QUESTIONS

Larry Myatt opened Fenway High School in 1983. It began as an alternative school-within-a-school in a large, comprehensive Boston high school to meet the needs of students alienated from traditional studies. When I had the chance, in the second year of operation, to join Fenway High School, first as the assistant director and later as codirector, I knew that without an overarching philosophy—a clearly defined *way of approaching learning,* or what I have come to call a unifying framework—we would do no better than the teachers in my first school had done. We would, perhaps, raise scores on the now "new and improved" district test and spend lots of time (and money we didn't have) ensuring that we were all implementing the same test-prep material in the same manner so that our classrooms would be "teacher proof." In fact, if our students didn't do well on the tests, since we were all in sync in every classroom in the school, we could easily blame it on the students for not paying attention, since we knew *we* were all paying attention and doing exactly what our administrators told us to do. Ultimately, though, as I had seen before, we would wind up depleted and demoralized. I knew that to succeed as a pedagogical community, we needed to have *the power of a unifying framework.*

At Fenway, a unifying framework meant that we developed a shared vocabulary for describing learning that all students and teachers (and parents) used. Teachers would also use similar terms or criteria for evaluating student work. Teachers would move from simply being providers of information to acting as coaches, and stressing personalization—both in making the curriculum connect to students' experiences and in how teachers embraced students—would be an important feature.

ASKING QUESTIONS ABOUT WHAT'S MOST
IMPORTANT CAN CREATE A SCHOOL

How to create this essential unifying framework? My experience teaches me that the only way to start is to ask the right set of questions.

In a single school day, let alone over the course of an academic year, scores upon scores of questions arise—questions about scheduling, lunch, discipline, pedagogy, seating arrangements, curriculum, rules, after-school activities, testing, college preparation, mentoring, student support, tracking, and so on. These are all important, but there are so many of them, and so many decisions to be made, that we can easily lose sight of what's *most* important of all. Questions must move from a singular thrust about the way things are to multiple stories about what could be, from symptoms to causes, from the work of adults to the learning and experiences of students.

During my first year as assistant director of the fledging Fenway High School, I met periodically with Vito, my educational mentor, who knew how to listen and push me to discuss the school's progress by gently and firmly asking hard questions. My conversations with Vito ran a predictable course. I'd lead off by venting: I'm not doing enough. I'm not doing a good enough job at what I *am* doing. The faculty is frustrated by how the students never seem to care enough about school to do a really good job. When I finished my litany of frustrations and mea culpas, the two of us would discuss what evidence I had to prove that my students didn't care. One week my mentor's response took me by surprise. "But, Linda," he said with a glint in his eye, "the *questions* you are posing as a faculty are getting so much better!" Huh? He pointed out that, at the start of the year, most of our questions were managerial in nature, about "law enforcement." How to get kids to behave and take off their headphones in the lunchroom. How to get kids to do their homework. How to get parents to come to school events.

Our focus in the fall was squarely on blame: blaming the parents, blaming the kids, blaming ourselves as failing rule enforcers. And, as I see looking back on that time, I was right there with them, blaming myself for failing the teachers. As you might imagine, there was a palpable feeling of failure and its partner, resentment, in faculty meetings as we got all tripped up about homework compliance and asked whether we should fail kids who didn't or couldn't get their homework done. Our de facto unifying philosophy was: "We're failing: Let's get together and blame!" (Imagine that one on a poster!)

But now, just a few months later, we'd gotten to the point as a faculty where we were asking different kinds of questions altogether: Why do we give homework in the first place? Why is it important to us that parents come to school events? Are these events even engaging for parents? What are we trying to accomplish by asking students to take off their headphones? This last question, for instance, led us in a completely different direction, because we realized that in part we were trying to orchestrate a way for kids to socialize across the boundaries of race and class, but headphones set up a scenario where no one had to interact.

The questions teachers and principals ask determine the direction we take and the depth of dialogue we have. What I'll call the "first-level" questions typically concern what *they,* the kids or the parents, are and aren't doing, and especially about what *they're* doing "wrong." Even tired teachers can play the awful game of "name that failure" for hours. As leaders and principals know, groups of teachers seem inexorably drawn to this kind of talk, and it is often our difficult job to steer the conversation away from the failure spiral and toward second-level questions.

This second, deeper level of questioning concerns what *we* (the adults in the school) are or aren't doing and *why*. Ultimately, this kind of questioning leads us to ask what we do or don't stand for. "Second-level" questions dig deeper; they get to the heart of our values and grapple with the bigger ideas in play, the ideas that led most of us into this profession in the first place. Most of us didn't enter teaching because we love to harp on rules. We became educators because we love kids and we love ideas and wanted to transfer this love to children. Many of us went into teaching because we believe that education is the key lever for changing the status quo—especially in terms of equity and access.

The shift from first- to second-level discourse allows us the opportunity to step back, view an issue from a wider perspective, and begin to articulate what is important and why. Take our case of homework compliance. When the faculty at Fenway moved to second-level questioning, we asked ourselves: is homework meaningful? Yes, we initially decided, because we want kids to practice outside of school. But, the questioning continued: What if there is no space and time for many kids to do homework outside of school? What if many of our kids have to work a second job or babysit siblings? We had to discuss whether we thought it was fair to fail our kids because they weren't doing their homework. We had to grapple with one another through lengthy and difficult discussions and ask: what is our ultimate goal, anyhow? By asking this set of broader questions, we discovered that what we were really after was the discipline of "practice." Then our questioning proceeded on a different tack: Does it really matter *where* homework or practice work happens? Why don't we create an enrichment block where kids can practice in school? Given the circumstances of many of our students, don't we have an obligation to do so? This line of questioning revived our energy to confront the true problems in front of us and reinforced the reasons we went into education in the first place. This was the beginning stage for us of the development of a unifying framework. We were naming and then deciding on a common set of agreements or understandings about our approaches to teaching and learning, and to our students.

I love to ask new principals, "What questions are you and your faculty asking every day? Take a step back and consider: What do you want your graduates to know and be able to do? And, perhaps most important, what has been denied to your students previously because of issues of race, class, gender, or language?" Mostly, I want principals to truly consider both when they find themselves knocking their heads against the wall, and then when they know how to turn that around into asking "what do we all care about *together* as a school community?" If we as leaders don't take the time to ask ourselves and each other questions like these, questions that give us a throughline and unifying framework that everyone can work toward, we are likely to wind up where the Fenway faculty was at the start of the year, chasing our tails through the failure spiral and running ourselves ragged all over the map.

THE POWER OF A UNIFYING FRAMEWORK

I first experienced the power of a unifying framework at Fenway High School. The school was built on the philosophy of putting student engagement first. At Fenway, we called our unifying framework "Habits of Mind." We wanted students and staff to practice certain ways of thinking in all of their classes. The term "habits of mind" didn't start with us; it was first coined by the philosopher John Dewey in the nineteenth century and later popularized in the mid-1980s by educators such as Deborah Meier, then director of Central Park East Secondary School (CPESS) in New York City.

The ways of thinking we wanted to focus on are captured in the acronym PERCS: *perspective, evidence, relevance, connection,* and *supposition.* At Fenway, we asked a particular set of questions: What is my *perspective* on this? What *evidence* do I have? What is the *rel-*

evance? What other *connections* can I make? And *suppose* that...?
Students had to apply a Habits of Mind framework to school projects
and exhibitions, even to homework. The PERCS framework we de-
vised worked well at Fenway.

I had first seen this framework in operation during visits to
CPESS. Sitting in on students' portfolio presentations in fourteen
different subject areas (including math, science, humanities, arts,
and service learning) I had been struck by the facility with which
faculty and students (and parents) used a common vocabulary for
discussing work and asking questions. As we adopted the framework
and made it ours at Fenway, we insisted that students use each aspect
of PERCS in their approach to all of their subjects. We reduced the
number of presentations or exhibitions from fourteen to five (math,
science, world languages, humanities, and Senior Project).

For each graduation exhibition, students spoke with confidence
about their perspective on a given topic, and how and why they had
arrived at this perspective. Students had to show evidence or proof
for their statements, and in discussions teachers and peers would ask
about relevance and connections. The Senior Project, which involved
a six-week-long internship, was a powerful opportunity to discuss relevance and connections. A student placed in a legal aid office could
begin to develop her passion for youth advocacy. The connection to
her own life and experiences was immediate, particularly because so
many of her friends were already involved in the court system. Supposition was always the most difficult habit. Teachers asked questions like: "Suppose that the author had ended the book differently?"
and "Suppose that history had taken another course?" Even though
some of the habits didn't feel as authentic or comfortable to use, Fenway has been using this framework to guide teaching and learning
for over twenty-five years now.

When I had the chance to start BAA, I assumed we could adopt
PERCS outright. I was wrong. The BAA faculty rejected the termi-

nology—not because they didn't passionately believe in the power
and importance of a unifying framework, but because the term "habits of mind" was too constricting for an arts school: we needed a
framework that captured both intellectual and creative work. This
debate over semantics, which may sound esoteric or technical, was
essential to our development as a faculty and our commitment to the
framework. Further, faculty insisted that our habits had to have their
genesis in arts terminology and the processes used by artists.

Disappointed but undaunted, I brought the faculty a new list
of terms, this time borrowed from the Harvard Graduate School of
Education's Project Zero: *collaboration, discipline, passion, risk-taking,
context, reflection,* and *foundation.* Since Project Zero is a renowned
research center that studies learning in arts classrooms, I was certain
that these terms would meet my faculty's criteria. Once again, I struck
out. My teachers rejected the Project Zero list. It wasn't that these
words were wrong or bad, but that they weren't *ours.* We needed to go
through our own lengthy process of constructing a framework before
we came up with a set of words we could all sign onto. We didn't want
a checklist of empty slogans that would wind up hanging unnoticed
on classroom bulletin boards. We wanted a framework that would
give meaning and *living* direction to our entire school community.
We knew that the terms we chose would help shape the kind of intellectual and artistic community to which we wanted to belong. At
the end of two years, after hours of faculty debate and discussion, we
decided on the habits of RICO: *refine, invent, connect,* and *own.*

So what do these terms mean, exactly? And, more importantly,
how do they get lived out in practice? We attached questions to each
term to help clarify for students—and for ourselves—how to approach teaching and learning. After inviting student input and brainstorming more than a dozen questions for each term, we honed the
list to two key questions per habit.

Refine. Have I conveyed my message? What are my strengths and weaknesses?

Invent. What makes this work inventive? Do I take risks and push myself?

Connect. Who is the audience and how does the work connect? What is the context?

Own. Am I proud of the work I am doing? What do I need to be successful?

The order of the terms was not critical, but the faculty liked the acronym RICO and so did our students. It is a useful mnemonic device. As we began to apply our new habits, we noticed that a school-wide conversation about learning was beginning. The habits crept into classrooms. Teachers decided, in the spirit of *refine,* to give students the chance to rewrite papers and retake tests as many times as needed to "get it right." Often, a high-level math assignment requires students to *invent* a unique problem that used concepts from class work. In order to *connect,* students link their arguments to evidence from other sources. Students practice *owning* their work when teachers routinely ask them to describe what they are proud of and where their work needs to be better. Of course, it was difficult for students to analyze what they needed to do to be more successful, especially when "work harder" was not a sufficient answer! But as they practice the habit of ownership, students often articulate insights about their own work that no teacher could provide for them.

HOW CAN A UNIFYING FRAMEWORK BE PUT INTO PRACTICE?

Now that we had defined the terms of our unifying framework, we had to begin the hard work of actually applying it. At first, every teacher in every class assigned RICO portfolios, which were a collection of assignments that illustrated one or more of the habits (refine, invent, connect, or own). Assignments might be a final project in math with a written reflection that described the process of doing the problems, or a research paper with multiple drafts, or a test a student had revised in order to improve a grade. Usually portfolios included projects that students had worked on over a period of time, or that the student felt demonstrated significant learning. As a result, students accumulated reams of documents demonstrating their RICO habits. It sounded great, but by the end of four years we were drowning in paperwork, and I wasn't sure that students paid any more attention to their RICO portfolios than they had to my weekly math tests, which I always found tossed in the trash after I handed them back.

The staff was not disenchanted with RICO as a framework, but we were frustrated with our cumbersome way of implementing it. We couldn't figure out what to do with all the RICO portfolios from each distinct classroom and subject area. Math or science teachers could end up with four years' worth of a student's portfolio sitting in boxes or file folders somewhere in their rooms, collecting dust. We wanted RICO to live in our school and not just be a slogan, without becoming a beast that burdened us. After some discussions, we decided to introduce midyear and end-of-year RICO portfolios to replace the subject-based portfolios. Students had to select assignments from a variety of classes, which they believed best represented their developing abilities to refine, invent, connect, and own their work. The midyear and end-of-year portfolios would culminate in a RICO review conducted with the student, her advisor, another faculty member as an observer, and often a parent.

Later in our school's development, we also introduced another kind of review process called the Sophomore Benchmark, modeled on a traditional "critique" used by arts colleges. We wanted students to experience an intense artistic review midway through their high school career for two reasons. First, faculty wanted students to commit to being an artist and a scholar at BAA. Second, if students had not met the required standard, they and their teachers and parents would have a chance to map out what additional arts classes the student needed to take in the summer, or to figure out together what other supports the school could offer.

The faculty also decided that our capstone graduation experience would be the Senior Project. All students, beginning in their junior year, develop a proposal that demonstrates their academic and artistic training over their four years and also addresses a community need. The project directs their knowledge and passion toward a practical cause and delivers experience as independent artists. Their final presentations must demonstrate artistic rigor, feasibility, and mutual benefit, as well as writing technique and presentation skills. In a Senior Project Fair, representatives from the community, universities, organizations, and artists review the proposals. They allocate funding for those who score in the top 20 percent. Some projects have included original choreography on the theme of eating disorders for young girls, a publicly designed mural project, a monologue performed to raise awareness of homeless teens, a steel-drum workshop at a local hospital, and a film on the effects of rape.

The next vignettes demonstrate how RICO, the Sophomore Benchmark, and the Senior Project work as a unifying framework at BAA and have become synonymous with what the school stands for.

HOW DO REAL LIVE STUDENTS AND THEIR TEACHERS USE THE UNIFYING FRAMEWORK?

1. Christina's RICO review

Bruno Rodriguez sits with his advisee, eleventh-grade music major Christina Nguyen, for her end-of-year review. Wearing a suit, a crisply ironed blouse, and dress shoes, Christina has heeded her advisor's instructions that these reviews are formal occasions. Her long hair, dyed red a few months ago and returning now to its original jet-black color, falls across the side of her face, partially obscuring one eye. Christina shuffles her folders in front of her and looks up at Mr. Rodriguez and another teacher, Anne Clark, whose job it is to take notes during the review.

These notes will be part of Christina's assessment folder and will be used as a basis for checking her progress in her senior year. I am also an observer. I try to sit in on different advisors' reviews each year. Since RICO is our "final exam," I want firsthand knowledge of how different teachers (and students and parents) experience this yearly exit requirement. I want to have a good sense of where we need to improve.

When Christina's mother arrives, Mr. Rodriguez directs her to a seat and extends a warm welcome. "Mrs. Nguyen, we are so glad you are here."

Mr. Rodriguez explains the purpose of the RICO review process required of all ninth-, tenth-, and eleventh-graders. This is a formal opportunity for Christina to be specific and honest about her progress throughout the academic year, and about how she hopes to improve in the future. All adults present, including Mrs. Nyugen, may comment and ask questions.

Mr. Rodriguez adds two crucial points: "Christina cannot fail this review. A student only fails by not showing up or not being prepared. And I want to remind everyone that this is not a time to criticize Christina or be upset with her for what she hasn't done, but rather to reflect on what she has done."

Mrs. Nguyen nods her head, but looks nervous. She twists her pocketbook strap, her eyes focused on the floor. Although she sits next to her daughter, there seems to be a great distance between them.

Mr. Rodriguez turns his attention to Christina and the review begins. "What have you brought to show us, Christina, that demonstrates the habit *refine*?" Christina immediately opens her purple folder and spreads out ten different pages of music, peppered with time signatures, sharps, flats, and notes.

"This is my first stab at a composition," she says, pointing to the first sheet. "It's really basic. The melody is simple and it stays within four-four time. As I got more comfortable, you can see how I refined this piece, even changing the key and time signature." Christina points to another sheet. "On this other version, I experimented more with the melody and added more accidentals, sharps, and flats. Then, in this last version, I add other instrumentation. I'm a pianist, but I added a flute here since I can hear this played with a wind instrument, too."

Mr. Rodriguez reviews the sheets and hands them to Ms. Clark.

"Impressive, Christina." Ms. Clark smiles. "Clearly your work with Ms. Lundberg has paid off. I remember that two years ago you didn't even read music."

"Perhaps when we finish here," Mr. Rodriguez suggests to Christina, "we can go next door and you can play this composition?"

"That would be fine, but it would just be the piano part." Christina smiles shyly.

"I have a question about this work," Mr. Rodriguez continues. "I'm curious why you have this composition to demonstrate *refine* as opposed to *invent*? You have so clearly pushed yourself with this score, which is the way we describe *invent*. To me *refine* is more about how you convey your message and show your understanding of your strengths and weaknesses, too."

"To me this is *refine*," says Christina. "I'm always inventing music, but refining takes more discipline for me. I can stay up till one or two in the morning inventing, but refining is something I have to really work at."

The review continues. Christina pulls out her *invent* folder and displays her Math 3 project in which she has demonstrated knowledge of quadratic equations by comparing prices and profit margins from three local stores that sell CDs.

"Was this the assignment from the class?" Mr. Rodriguez asks.

"No, no," Christina explains. "We were studying quadratics and profit margins in class. But I came up with this scenario about the stores."

To demonstrate *connect*, Christina discusses the poetry she wrote in writing seminar and explains how her poems connect with the haikus and sonnets she studied in class. "I loved writing the haikus," Christina explains with confidence. "I liked the rigidity of the style. It was kind of like writing music for me."

For the fourth and final habit, *own*, the discussion shifts to Christina's difficulties in Spanish class. In this case, she talks less about owning her work than owning her lack of it. She displays her final, incomplete Spanish project on the writer Rubén Darío. "I just can't write well in Spanish, even though I liked learning about this poet. I've failed for the second year in a row. I know it's a graduation requirement and I'm a junior, but I just don't like the class." Christina resorts to complete honesty: "I end up skipping more than I go, and that's why I failed."

Mr. Rodriguez nods. In her midyear RICO conference, Christina had signed a formal contract, along with her mother and the Spanish teacher, stipulating steps for improvement, including a promise to attend daily classes.

"I know the contract was supposed to help me," Christina says. "I just didn't feel like going all semester."

"Let me ask you a question, Christina." Mr. Rodriguez pauses. "What are you doing *right* in your piano and composition class that might help you out in Spanish?"

Christina thinks for a moment before replying. "Well, I know that I am always willing to put in the effort in music to make the piece better."

Mr. Rodriguez then maps out a consequence. Christina will have to attend summer school for Spanish, an outcome that may create a conflict with her desire to attend a summer program at the renowned Berklee College of Music.

Mr. Rodriguez asks Christina one final question about her goals for senior year. Christina responds carefully, while Ms. Clark transcribes. "Well, I certainly need to learn to go to class, especially Spanish. I want to graduate next June. I know I'm smart enough to pass all my classes if I just go. So I guess what I have to learn is to make myself do stuff even when I don't like it. Otherwise, I pay for it later."

"I would say that's true," Mr. Rodriguez says, and then asks Christina's mother if she'd like to make any comments.

In halting English Mrs. Nguyen thanks him for taking care of her daughter and looking out for her all year. "I know she will do better in Spanish," she says. "I am sorry for that." Then she comments on her daughter's music. "I don't ever understand. She shuts her door. She has earphones on. She is playing on the keyboard all the time. I tell her to go to bed so she is not so tired. But she doesn't listen. I didn't realize she writes music. I didn't know she was so good. I don't play. Her grandfather, in Vietnam, played. I am proud." She pats Christina's arm. "This will give her a scholarship to college? This is good."

"She is very good," Mr. Rodriguez agrees. "And I feel that she understands her challenges for next year. You *should* be very proud of her, Mrs. Nguyen. Let's go listen to this composition."

The original music, at once forceful and eerie, sounds both Western and Asian in origin. When Christina concludes, she seems almost out of breath. She sits quietly.

Ms. Clark is the first to speak. "Christina, it makes me want to practice *my* flute so I can play it with you!"

Christina smiles. "When we come back to school, okay? I'll give you a copy of the music so you can learn it."

Mrs. Nguyen turns to her daughter. "Maybe now I won't yell at you for all the time you spend in your room. Now I understand what you do there. Your grandfather, he would be so proud."

Christina gathers up her music. The review is over.

In Christina's review, while I saw that she generally understood the terms and was very persuasive discussing her skills at refining her composition, I was perplexed that she, now an eleventh-grader familiar with RICO reviews, chose a rather simple extension of a math problem. She claimed that her scenario about the store showed invention, but I didn't feel it demonstrated an extension or deepening of her math skills in any significant way. I wondered how good a job we were really doing with implementing RICO assignments in all classes.

Still, in the area of *own*, I was pleased that Christina recognized how the habits she had learned through her music studies could transfer to her Spanish class. In the review she began to *own* the fact that passing Spanish was under her control, and that she must pass the class if she wanted to achieve her dream of going to Berklee College of Music. This showed me that for Christina, the student-school relationship had shifted from one of mutual blame to one of alliance for success. Of course it doesn't always work like that, and it is not always so seamless. Even though Christina did demonstrate some significant ownership of her own learning, she still had not demonstrated positive results in Spanish. Her proficiency was not at the level that teachers would have wished, even though her ability to be reflective about her roadblocks was impressive.

Later, when I had the chance to debrief the review with Mr. Rodriguez and Ms. Clark, we agreed that we were only semi-successful with Christina. We want students to demonstrate mastery in all subject areas, not to merely throw a math extension together and use the RICO words. Our goal is for students to articulate actions that can change their behaviors. But we are not always successful in the moment. (Christina, in fact, had to forfeit her place in the Berklee summer program to attend summer school for Spanish.) RICO reviews may help with reflection but they cannot create miracles.

Nevertheless, I feel that the time we spend on the reviews is well worth it. It gives us a way to talk about student work and ultimately become better teachers. It gives us a method to discuss and recommit to our core beliefs—our overarching framework. Yes, it requires endless hours of meetings, and leads to many disagreements, but ultimately I believe that our students learn more.

2. Gerry's Sophomore Benchmark

Gerry perches on a stool in front of his assembled work, waiting for his review panel to begin. Kathleen Marsh, the head of the department; Beth Balliro, another visual arts teacher; Marcos, an eleventh-grade student; and I take our seats in the small classroom. Ms. Marsh frames the session: "So, Gerry, this is your Sophomore Benchmark. We are going to review how you feel you have demonstrated 'seriousness of purpose' in your work—how you bring your whole self to a project with honesty and integrity." With that introduction, Ms. Marsh pulls up her tall frame, adjusts her glasses, and extends her arms widely to take in the work, all of us, and especially Gerry. "Let's begin by looking at the two self-portraits you've brought."

Gerry sits completely still, listening intently. He looks at his two self-portraits—one from ninth grade and one from tenth grade—that rest on the easels in the room. Describing the work, Gerry notes his improvement with proportion from one year to the next, and his use of shading, light, and texture.

Ms. Marsh pushes him to be even more specific. She picks up one of the portraits. "What about the use of value and color of your skin? How do you show how the light hits your face? What happens to the places the light hits and the places the light doesn't hit?"

Gerry hesitates. "I tried to make my cheeks lighter because they are smooth and more light hits them. I knew that my nostrils and top of my lips should be darker cause not as much light gets there. I tried to do that," Gerry replies.

"What about inside your nostrils? What is happening there?" Ms. Marsh persists.

Gerry doesn't answer. He just looks more keenly at the portrait. Ms. Marsh tries to help. "What can you say about light or darkness *inside* the nostril?"

Gerry seems to get her point. "Not enough light gets there so it's supposed to be very dark. I didn't really do it dark enough, though. I could've done better. I didn't work at refining enough times. And, I'm not sure I was being too inventive. Portraits really aren't my thing," he says dismissively.

The review then turns to an examination of the three-dimensional object Gerry has brought—his Batman sculpture. Ms. Marsh asks him to talk about what he would have done differently, technically.

Gerry is more at ease here. "I really worked hard on this, but I would have hollowed it out more so it wouldn't have fallen in. See how the head caved in a bit? If I'd have hollowed it out, I don't think that would've happened when it was fired. This was also the first time we worked with high fire glazes."

Ms. Marsh and Ms. Balliro both agree that they can see he tried hard and is successful in communicating to the viewer that he thinks Batman is cool.

"It is really cool," Marcos, the student participant, interjects. "I wish I could work with clay like that. I think you'll get better with portraits, too, after you practice more. You do Batman's nose really well and you can learn to do that on a two-dimensional drawing."

"I don't know," Gerry says somewhat glumly. "My hands know what to do when I'm working with clay, but when I have a pencil or charcoal I have to work too hard and there's too much to think about it. I know I'm not as good as everyone else in the class."

As the review of the actual artwork finishes up, Ms. Marsh transitions to the goal setting part of the session.

"So what do you want to get better at for next year?" Ms. Marsh asks.

"I need to get my work in on time. I need to have more motivation. I've always had a problem with that, especially when I think it's a waste of time or I don't like it," he says.

Ms. Balliro counters, "But you'll never like everything you do in school. How do you get motivated when you don't like something? What do you do when you are not excited about something? How do you find excitement?"

Gerry looks at them. He sighs quietly, maybe a bit sadly. "I don't know. I've had a hard time with that for a long time."

"Well," Ms. Marsh prods, "what have you learned from your growth in visual arts that you could apply to your academic classes?"

Gerry shifts uncomfortably.

Marcos speaks up, breaking the tension. "I know for me, I had a big breakthrough when I started sketching on the train. You have a long commute, too, right? I'd just put my headphones on and I'd zone out and zone in to doing the homework exercises. Pretty soon, even I could see improvements. And then, somehow, that helped me shift into a better place in class. I just felt more confident."

"Yeah, that's what it is—confidence and practice. They sort of go together. Hard to have one without the other. I'm seeing that more now. I know I'd be more motivated if I did the work. Kind of obvious I guess," Gerry says quietly.

"So that's great, Gerry," Ms. Marsh sums up. "Let's see if we can begin to make that recognition into some goals and action steps for next semester." She pulls out a paper that is divided into sections— semester one and two with headings of Goals and Action Steps. Together they begin to fill out the sheet. "Here we'd put, 'daily practice in sketchbook,' right?"

"Yeah, I like Marcos's idea. I can do that on the T."

"Let's put under Action Steps 'sketch on T.' " Ms. Marsh writes as Gerry talks through his goals and action steps for the following year.

By the time the official Sophomore Benchmark ends, Gerry has been pushed and prodded by teachers and peers to look closely at his own progress and to set achievable goals. He has been asked to think about specific examples of where he's been successful and where he still feels frustrated. It is easy to set a broad goal like, "Pass all my classes," but it's harder to set a specific goal like, "Sketch for forty-five minutes on the T." The skills of self-reflection, self-assessment, and goal setting that Gerry is learning will help him in both his arts and academic classes at BAA, as well as in college and throughout his life.

After both Gerry and Marcos had left the room, Ms. Marsh and Ms. Balliro conferred and agreed that Gerry's skills were not strong enough to move on to the eleventh-grade level. He would need to repeat the sophomore year in visual arts. They would schedule another meeting with him and a parent to break this news.

Perhaps at another high school, Gerry might have gone mindlessly through the motions of school, hoping to just get by. He might have been secretly grateful for the chaos, confusion, and disconnectedness of his high school experiences because they would have enabled him to remain anonymous and unnoticed. But Gerry would be the first to say that while his Sophomore Benchmark sometimes made him squirm, it also made him think hard about what he wants to accomplish during the next two years of high school and even beyond. Although he was very disappointed when he learned that he would need to repeat the year in arts class, he also knew that his skills were not up to par compared to those of his classmates. He knew that this meant that he would not be able to graduate on time, and although he tried to negotiate to take an arts class in summer school, his department stood firm: he would repeat the year in his arts major.

The results of Gerry's benchmark reflect hard choices that teachers, parents, students, and I have made about the importance of really understanding material and being "good enough." As a school that specializes in the arts, we have decided that we must draw this kind of clear line in the sand. It has not been easy, but it has taught me the importance of asking the questions: Do the minimum standards at my school truly measure what we want them to measure? And, if a student is not meeting them, what are the ways in which we support his learning? The Sophomore Benchmark, in particular, makes it impossible for a capricious decision to be made about a student's future since there must be departmental consensus.

I believe it was worth it for Gerry to hang in there and learn the requisite skills. There was no failure attached to Gerry's work, but rather an acknowledgment that for some students it will take longer to graduate and include summer school, night school, or an extra year.

3. "Love of My Life": Melanie's Senior Project

The Senior Project, which is BAA's capstone experience, helps students develop an idea all the way to its implementation stage. Although not all students actually implement their project during high school, many do so after they start college. RICO is the organizing framework for the project. Students begin project development in their junior year and then refine their ideas through a carefully structured process until presentation in the fall of the senior year. Each project is also judged on its inventiveness, the degree to which students connect to their proposed ideas, and, of course, how they demonstrate ownership.

Melanie is hoping her project, "Love of My Life," will be funded. She describes how her project builds a bridge for her back to her community. "Teens need a place where they can be themselves, and also figure out who they are—their identities." Melanie stands barely five feet tall. She is wearing elegant high heels, two-toned red shoes that match her suit, and a ribbon in her hair. Her dark skin glows against her outfit. She explains to the reviewers how she will work in an after-school program in a very under-resourced section of the city to give teens the opportunity to take vocal technique and theater improvisation classes that culminate in a short musical. She stands before her display board that is complete with lesson plans, a time line, and a budget, and speaks with passion about her proposal:

> "I have learned over my four years here a lot about technique and how to use the body and the face to communicate that technique. I did a few musical scenes from Gilbert and Sullivan; I also learned some Broadway numbers, and I'm working on an Italian aria now. We've also done some popular music over the years. I will be able to teach young people the connection between the voice and the body. The students will keep a journal that will contain different prompts that elaborate on their experiences.

> "Students will also choose songs that relate to those experiences. Everyone listens to performers like Alicia Keys, and rappers speak to many life experiences. I've learned that people like Gustav Mahler, who most kids have never heard of, also wrote about pain and suffering the same way that Kanye West or Billie Holiday did. We will spend part of each class also learning about different music.

> "Students will write monologues based on writing prompts. Then they develop characters through improvisation and through song. Then we will rehearse how students will ex-

press themselves through their monologues and the songs they have chosen. We will perform these scenes at the local community center or the church."

Finally Melanie explains the rationale for her project. "Young adolescents need the opportunity to be a positive asset to their community. I know firsthand how easy it is to be brought down by the bad things going on around you or in your family or your community. The goal of this program is to give the youth a place of refuge from the negativity of society and also to teach them how to safely express themselves."

Melanie recognizes what so many school or policy officials seem to forget—the arts are a powerful force to help change our world, and most young people can make an immediate connection between the arts and popular culture. Melanie's project is also helping her develop academic skills in reading, writing, oral presentation, and even basic mathematics. She had to develop a budget and figure out what resources can be considered "in-kind," since she is learning early on the lesson that there is never enough money. And she had to revise her proposal at least four times until she got it up to the required standard. She had to read her proposal aloud and commit much of it to memory or note cards in order to stand before outsiders who will determine if she is deserving of funding. RICO, the unifying framework of the school, is evident in every aspect of her proposal.

WHAT HAS THE RICO FRAMEWORK DONE FOR OUR SCHOOL IN A LARGER SENSE?

The RICO habits, the Sophomore Benchmark, and the Senior Project at BAA have become a practical way for teachers, students, and parents to define our standards for passing work. These opportunities for students and teachers, and often parents, to be vulnerable and reflective with one another create the possibilities for a school community to go beyond slogans to become an intellectual and creative community.

Both Christina and Gerry's reviews show that at BAA we have "put our money where our mouth is," so to speak. It is much more costly, in terms of both time and money to do these individual student-advisor or student-department reviews. Our schedule accommodates RICO reviews, Sophomore Benchmarks, and Senior Projects. Additionally, students need opportunities to present to literally hundreds of adults for their Senior Projects, and this requires extensive organization on the part of the faculty. We have had to allocate time for advisors to contact parents, and time for teachers to talk about how the reviews or Senior Project went and what we can improve for the following year. There is no point in involving outsiders to critique our student work if their comments aren't taken seriously. The effort is worth it in terms of how our students truly "own" their learning and how all of us know what our school stands for. We are clear, all of us, that mastery is neither a random act nor an innate gift. Rather, it is the result of well-disciplined habits. Those habits define who we are, as well as our aspirations for who our students will become.

Although the faculty at BAA is still searching for a more streamlined approach to implementing the reviews, we are confident of their value. Because the invention of RICO reviews and the benchmark developed out of our original ideas about what mattered to us as a school, we don't need to throw them away and go running off after the next hot idea presented at a conference, hoping that this one will work. We are clear about *what* we want to do and *why*. *How* is a question we can tackle again and again without having to question our sense of direction.

And with the Senior Project we see the power of our students being taken seriously by an adult world where they soon will participate. Melanie, and others like her, embodies the best of what a unifying framework offers in a school: she has shown us how education can connect to a young person's life and experiences and be completely engaging.

Am I arguing that every successful school has to have in place a set of "Habits of the Graduate," such as RICO, or a review process like the Sophomore Benchmark, or a Senior Project? Of course not. I have visited schools that have no acronym like RICO or PERCS, but excel at making learning and assessment transparent to everyone. Leaders in many schools, hoping to address these problems and change the way their students experience school, may have initiated programs, such as an advisory system, a block schedule, portfolio assessment, or small learning communities. One such school, which I'll call Central Middle School, requires all students to do an eighth-grade Graduation Exhibition in which students discuss their learning and growth throughout their three years by reading an excerpt from their autobiography, sharing their science fair project, and doing an extension of a math problem. Younger students, other classroom teachers, adult community members, and often a parent sit in as jury members to assess whether a student is qualified to graduate. In addition, each student is prepared to answer questions. It is often in this question and answer period that a student's true comprehension of the work shines forth. This exhibition is their unifying framework.

Everyone at Central can talk about the importance of the Graduation Exhibition. Students are given multiple chances to redo it, and there have only been a few cases where students have had to go to summer school to finish up requirements. The Graduation Exhibition is part of the lived fabric of Central. All students, parents, teachers, and administrators work toward this final right of passage. The exhibition is introduced as soon as students begin in sixth grade, and all classes and grades work on it. The Graduation Exhibition stands in stark contrast to schools where students experience school as a race to pass a series of fairly meaningless classes or, worse, a succession of lessons in "what I did wrong today in school" or "what I didn't finish." At Central, teachers have found that mapping out ideals of *thinking and learning* as well as models of behavior, for both students and faculty, gives them a unity from which to talk about their practices and results.

Think about the school you work in, attend, or send your children to. These places are vital to us, no matter which role we are in. What learning and thinking habits are expected of this school's graduates? Are these habits expressed as a unifying framework? If not, what are the gaps between what the school purports to believe and actual lived practice? If your school has a framework, something like "High Expectations for All," how is that expressed as part of the school's mission and in daily classroom practices? How do you know as a teacher, a principal, a parent, or a student that this framework is practiced everywhere? If you find yourself unable to answer these questions, or notice that you are groping for the "right" answers, it is probably a sign that the school isn't succeeding at its mission, no matter how high its average SAT or state scores, which prizes its graduates have won, how large its library is, or how many of its students go to prestigious colleges.

I am suspicious of statements that begin with "All schools should..." But this is one I truly stand behind: all schools should develop and use a unifying framework. The "new initiative every year" model doesn't work. Teachers need to be involved in articulating the framework, and a school *must* be willing to commit to the implementation of the framework over the long haul. Finally, I would argue that schools without a unifying framework still have an unspoken one—a de facto assumption of what this school is about. If it were expressed in posters on the wall, these frameworks might be "We Are Failing: Who Should We Blame?" or "High Scores and College

Admissions—Everything Else Be Damned!" To honestly answer the question "What does your school stand for?" takes a willingness to ask again and again how your practices are improving, what students know and can do, and how day-to-day realities in the classroom match the ideals you have articulated.

2.

What Happens When Schools Develop Shared Values?

What can school leaders do when those values are challenged?

THE "WHITE POWER" INCIDENT

In the spring of 2002 the entire school gathered for an emergency assembly. Someone had written on the wall of one of the boys' bathrooms the words "White Power" and had drawn a swastika. Although I like to think I believe in "innocent until proven guilty," I immediately began to think about which student might have done such a thing.

After a quick consultation with Ms. Torres, the assistant principal, I decided to interrupt classes. As school leaders, we knew we needed to express our zero-tolerance policy for hate speech in any public place and especially in our school. We had to enlist the larger community, students, and teachers, in discussing how to address this act of hate and vandalism. We quickly caucused with the head of student support and our school police officer. Both agreed that this was a serious incident that merited immediate attention. Although a few teachers were visibly grumpy about losing class time for such an assembly, for the most part everyone rose to the occasion and accompanied their classes to the cafeteria—the only space large enough to hold all four hundred and fifteen students plus faculty. I noticed a few students snickering as they sat down. I thought, suspiciously, that these might be the very ones who could enjoy the negative attention that such an act of vandalism can bring.

Ms. Torres and I stood before the entire school. I tried not to look at the students I was most suspicious of. I spoke first. "We are sorry to pull you from classes. You have heard me say many times that you have a right to your education, and I hate to have you lose class time, but we needed to share a terrible thing that has happened in our school." I knew my voice was trembling with pent-up emotion as I explained what had happened. "Whoever did this may have been a coward, a troubled prankster, or a very mean person, or all of those things. The person or people may never identify themselves, but I feel strongly that as a community we all need to take responsibility and respond to this abomination." I wanted to continue, but I knew I was too angry to speak anymore.

Ms. Torres picked up where I had left off. "We have decided to cancel last period classes. Everyone will go to his or her advisory groups. We will come around to distribute some prompts for your discussion." Advisory is a small group of eight to ten students from all grades (ninth through twelfth) that meets four times a week for about fifteen minutes with a teacher. The purpose of advisory is to have all students known well by one adult, as well as to be a place where students can share both successes and struggles in a nonjudgmental, supportive atmosphere.

An outpouring of emotions and ideas followed. Most students were appalled at this invasion into their seemingly safe and loving community. Students wrote and spoke about how as artists and scholars they were in a privileged position to fight against racism and hatred. They expressed their fears that their school might be harboring hate-mongers. Some wrote openly about how BAA always had seemed safer than the streets, but that now they were afraid for their personal safety. Others questioned whether we would have expressed the same outrage over the term "black power" on the walls.

An eleventh-grader told us that she believed that racist actions were due to the behavior of parents and the way they brought up their kids. She hoped that the school would hold many more productive meetings about tolerance with the individual or individuals, once they were identified, and added, "We need to keep talking about this in advisory groups." Many students shared their own experiences with hatred, discrimination, and prejudice.

Teachers wrote, too. Most said that this act of desecration required more than one assembly, plus follow-up discussions and writing assignments in advisory. "It's not enough to just discuss this once. We all know that these issues are right under the surface, and we need to have time to discuss both the anger and the fear we all feel," one teacher wrote. For weeks after the event, students and staff came to me with suggestions for further action. Some suggested we should spend time going over our Community Standards so that students would understand acceptable behavior as the school defines it. Our Community Standards outlined our policies on everything from sexual harassment and appropriate attire to weapons and drugs, and clearly laid out the consequences of violating these policies. Perhaps, faculty suggested, we should teach a required unit or units that focused on various teen and social issues. Students suggested that we think about support groups or even identity groups so that people would feel safe talking about their life experiences with racism and hatred. We posted everyone's responses on a large bulletin board titled "Student Responses to Community with Social Responsibility." This phrase became BAA's first Shared Value, and we eventually spelled out three more. Whereas RICO was a framework for approaching teaching and learning and the attitudes we wanted students to bring to all their work, Shared Values spoke to a different aspect of our community—how we interacted with one another and the world.

Soon after we had coined the first value, we held a faculty meeting to discuss our responses to it. Mr. Mendes, a special education teacher, began by offering his suggestion about how to integrate this value into our school lives. "I think community with responsibility begins with all of us agreeing to say no to hats, iPods, and do-rags. And cell phones. Community with responsibility means nothing if we aren't all on board with the rules. How can teachers look the other way when students are walking down the hallways bopping to their music? I just don't get that. If the rules mean something we have to uphold them." He glared at his colleagues, daring them to disagree. Some teachers rolled their eyes.

"Are we really having this conversation again?" Mr. Wade spoke for a number of teachers. "How many years am I going to have to sit and talk about gum and hats? I honestly don't think it has anything to do with learning. I'm sorry, Jose," Mr. Wade spoke directly to Mr. Mendes.

Jose countered. "Roland, you know that's *not* what I'm talking about. I'm talking about how we are not united as an adult community. I don't think we can expect students to live values that we can't agree on. If we ignore students who flagrantly break the rules, what does that say about us? We have to be consistent."

The conversation went a few more rounds. Finally, I broke in. "Look, we could talk about hats, gum, iPods, and cell phones forever. Many of us feel that when students are plugged-in or not respectable-looking that they aren't ready to learn. Some of you feel hats and do-rags are an issue of respect. Others feel very strongly about gum chewing. For others of you, it's just not a big deal. Basically, what I hear you saying is that if we have rules, we should enforce them. I would agree.

"But I'd like to try and turn this discussion around and talk about how to capture a set of values that we can all commit to. Then, we need to ask ourselves how to make those shared values real to our students and parents. Does a rule against hats or gum really represent a shared value? Is this what we mean when we say 'community with responsibility'? Or does it represent something else?"

We entered into lengthy discussions, just as we had done with the terms for RICO, at both faculty meetings and leadership team meetings, and eventually, we articulated four Shared Values:

Passion with Balance
Vision with Integrity
Community with Social Responsibility
Diversity with Respect

Our first understanding of "passion with balance" came from a need, as we adults saw it, to teach students to respond passionately while balancing that passion with appropriate behavior. In other words, we want students to understand that, for instance, calling out is a natural part of a hip-hop concert but disruptive in a classical piano recital. "Vision with integrity" means creating your own work while acknowledging those on "whose shoulders you stand." We expect students to have enough humility to credit the artists and genres that paved the way for them. We want them to understand that plagiarism is not just about copying someone else's writing. "Community with social responsibility" means taking care of one another in our community and paying attention to interactions in our school community and with the rest of the world. "Diversity with respect" means including all students, teachers, and families without prejudice related to background, culture, race, class, gender, language of origin, or sexual orientation.

Our Shared Values emerged from our need to decide on and commit to a definition of what it meant to be an individual within the greater BAA community and how we should interact with one another. We call these *Shared* Values as opposed to just "values," because we want these values to define what our entire community stands for.

Arising as it did out of a real-time school crisis, the initial struggle to articulate our Shared Values was in some respect a response to worries about our community and the attitudes and behaviors of our students. Every school leader has probably faced a similar situation and responded with outrage equal to my own. I think that the decision to widen and deepen the discussion about the "white power" incident marked a real turning point in our school community. It gave us a way to talk about behavioral expectations that complemented and enhanced RICO, and it forced us to recast our concerns as positive statements, rather than as prohibitions. We don't have an assembly every time a negative incident occurs, but we usually find a way to make the infractions part of our curriculum. I have come to realize that when I say to my students, "You have a right to an education here," I also mean that we will spend time, as we need to, discussing issues that threaten to knock us from the strong foundation of our shared values.

HOW CAN DEVELOPING SHARED VALUES HELP
US CHANGE THE DAILY LIFE OF A SCHOOL?

Many teenagers experience high school as a place where adults act *on* them, rather than a place for students to act *in* and belong to. Getting kids to buy into collective norms at the level of BAA's Shared Values has turned this situation on its head. Most BAA students, I'm happy to say, can demonstrate an understanding of at least one of the Shared Values.

As Shared Values became a way to talk about what was important in our community, and even the way to address some of our rules, a few students suggested that we change our quarterly honor-roll assemblies to be called Honor Roll/Shared Values assemblies. They wanted the school to recognize students when they were "Caught in the Act of Shared Values," a phrase they coined. Students or faculty could nominate students who had done something to exemplify a shared value. The action wouldn't have to be a big deal, but it had to be something that everyone could applaud. We have, for instance, acknowledged students "caught in the act" of putting up posters that someone had ripped down, staying behind to help clean up a classroom, bringing in doughnuts for everyone in the class after a strenuous day of testing, making sure the cafeteria tables were all wiped down, or even reminding their peers to take off their hats! I love the phrase "caught in the act" because it captures the idea that while rules are only acknowledged when they are broken, Shared Values can also make themselves known when they are demonstrated.

One year, after a number of teachers and students were the victims of repeated iPod and cell phone thefts, they formed a committee called "Community with Social Responsibility" at school and began an all-out campaign against theft. The slogan they introduced was, "I got you!" Meaning: "I got your back and I won't stand by and let stuff be stolen here anymore." More than three hundred students signed petitions and purchased "I got you!" stickers designed by visual arts students. In addition to the money raised (which went to support Pennies for Patients, a foundation for children with leukemia), the level of conversation, debate, and consciousness was raised to the point where it could be called a true movement. I can't say that BAA is now theft-proof, but today "I got you" permeates the hallways, and living the Shared Values is part of our daily lexicon.

I have visited other schools, particularly urban high schools, where it is the negative honor code of the street and the prohibitions of the administration that permeate life during the school week. Because these two codes are in direct opposition to one another, how can school leaders expect and demand conversations about *shared* values? How can students embrace school rules without feeling that they have to betray a set of values held by their peers?

Fenway High School's slogan—"Work Hard. Be Yourself. Do the Right Thing"—represents that school's shared values. Fenway students and faculty use this slogan as a way of exploring, defining, and redefining what is important in their community. Fenway alumni say that they learned these values in their coursework and from the school's conversations between faculty and students. The alumni continue to tell me about how they try to "do the right thing" whether in their work life, family life, or religious and community activities. BAA's Shared Values are fast becoming our way to hold before us all that which is essential and positive about our own community.

WHAT CAN LEADERS DO WHEN VALUES CLASH?

The Queer 101 incident

In some ways, the "white power" incident was simpler than other situations, because it didn't really provoke a moral conflict. No one in the school was going to stand up and say, "White power is right and we should have swastikas all over our walls!" Most school leaders believe in celebrating students' individual identities as members of a racial, cultural, gender, or linguistic group, as long as that isn't harmful to anyone else. Most school leaders would also say, "I think it is good to have something like a common set of shared values that have meaning beyond words." How that plays out in practice, however, can be exceedingly complex and unexpected. And often, I'm sorry to say, the shared values school leaders and teachers articulate are *not* tested or discussed—and the faculty goes back to the endless gum and hats discussions.

For instance, it is all well and good to say we believe in "diversity with respect," but until students (and teachers) can truly engage in open and honest debate about what such a belief means to them, these will be empty words. The danger is always that politically correct slogans will take the place of genuine moral thinking. A real, robust debate about diversity will emerge only when people are pushed to confront issues they are uncomfortable talking about.

From a practical standpoint, such debates take a tremendous amount of time and energy. School leaders like me get tired of pushing them, and teachers sometimes resist them as a "waste of time." But I continue pushing because I have seen such positive results come from the debates.

Early in our school's history, teachers and students at BAA identified homophobia as one of the most difficult issues to discuss. Several students came to me, angry and hurt because they felt that adults were brushing aside numerous small "gay bashing" incidents. A poster advertising a movie that the GSA (Gay-Straight Alliance) group was hosting after school had been torn down. Students were outraged, but no perpetrators were ever identified. Even after a school production of Moisés Kaufman's hard-hitting play *The Laramie Project,* which vividly portrays a real example of a young man murdered because of his open homosexuality, students were frustrated by the continued homophobia and apathy.

Some teachers also felt that we hadn't adequately addressed the issue. Mr. Malcolm spoke forcefully, "Look, it's time to take the blinders off! Nowhere in the three years that I've been here have we ever had any professional development about sexual orientation. Our students are thinking about this all the time, but we just do nothing." Almost challenging his peers, he went on, "I'm probably the only teacher here who students can come to, because I'm out!"

There was an uneasy silence in the room before Ms. Devine countered. "That's not fair to say. I think students talk to a lot of us about their identity issues—whether or not they think we are gay or straight. In fact, I don't think our personal sexual orientation has any bearing. Kids don't need to know about us personally; they just need to feel safe talking to us."

"No, I disagree. It's the twenty-first century now. I think kids deserve to know if their teachers are gay. It helps them realize it's normal. I talk about my husband all the time—just like you talk about yours," Mr. Malcolm returned. "I've been saying for a while that we are ignoring the fact that sexual orientation, particularly for our young men of color, may be a contributing factor to their lack of academic success."

I thought about all the questions that Mr. Malcolm's comments raised. I also knew that for some of our older or more traditional teachers, like Ms. Devine, keeping her personal life to herself was a key part of her sense of professionalism. Another teacher told me about a one-man show he had seen at an educational conference called Queer 101. He thought that seeing this play as a faculty would help move our conversations forward. I agreed that an artistic response to an emotional issue is a great idea, and invited the artist, Peterson Toscano, to perform for the faculty.

Using humor, Toscano tells original stories about the passion and confusion of Internet dating, conflicts and contradictions in the queer community today, the people who shaped queer history, and his own life's journey. Playing a variety of characters (including Audre Lourde, Langston Hughes, and Federico García Lorca), Toscano investigates themes of racism, homophobia, oppression, and power. In his "talk-back" with the audience after the show, Toscano identifies himself as an artist and a Christian, and discusses how his sexual orientation complicates for others his deep spiritual and religious beliefs and practices. He makes his audience feel the profound discrimination that he has experienced. He also educates everyone about the range of vocabulary used to describe what he calls "queer issues," and he does so while making the audience laugh. I had hoped that by watching Toscano's performance together, the BAA adult community could begin some tough but important conversations about homophobia, and this did indeed happen.

After lengthy faculty discussions about the show's messages, followed by ongoing work with Toscano, we decided it was important to bring the piece to students and parents the following fall. If teachers were uncomfortable, no one said anything. The Student Support team gave teachers guidelines for discussion prompts for advisory meetings. The main theme for prepping students for the performance was "diversity with respect" and how Toscano's piece might embody this value. Although we knew many students and parents had strong religious beliefs that condemned homosexuality, the faculty felt that it was critical to establish safety guidelines such as "no blame, shame, or attack." We were committed to holding and honoring differing ideas and opinions about homosexuality. Teachers made it clear that everyone was entitled to their own personal or religious beliefs, but no one had the right to publicly denigrate or demean anyone else. Embracing the value of "diversity with respect" meant being tolerant about many different kinds of differences.

Whether or not I agreed with Mr. Malcolm's accusations about achievement and young men of color, I feel strongly that homophobia, like racism, is a moral issue. Fortunately, the staff at BAA largely affirms this belief. I'm still not sure what I would have done if the dominant culture in our school faculty had disagreed. Would it have been right for me to use my power as a school leader to stand up for beliefs I held strongly, even if they were not shared? Even as difficult as this issue was for me, I know that many school leaders face even more agonizing choices as they balance their own moral convictions with the need to respect community standards.

We gave ourselves plenty of time to discuss with students the themes that would emerge in the performance. Since BAA opened, we have actively taught our students to sit as audience members in different kinds of performances and to think about appropriate responses. Now we had to help students get ready to respond appropriately to a performance that was bound to shake them up.

During the weeks leading up to the show, many students said things like, "I think being gay is just wrong," or "This goes against my religion," but agreed that they could attend the show and learn from it. We had discussions in advisory groups about how often art is about giving expression to values that may be strongly held by some and rejected by others. Sometimes it is this very conflict that an artist wants to explore. Teachers assured students that our intent was not to tell them what to believe, but to help them think carefully about the issue. One teacher summed it up well: "You are not being asked to approve of homosexuality if you do not, but you *are* being asked to pay attention and give the performer and your peers your respect."

I tried to engage in the same discussions with parents. At our back-to-school meetings in late August, I announced that we would bring the show to school and that we would have a special session with parents after the show. I explained that we were also preparing our students for the performance. I wrote in our monthly newsletter that I felt the show elucidated one of our Shared Values, and I talked about why I felt it was imperative to address controversial issues at school. I explained that no one had to change their opinion, but that we would require the audience to listen and be respectful. I did everything I could think of to avoid the problems that can come about when kids or parents are "blindsided" by an event they aren't prepared for.

And yet, on the day of the performance, I worried that students, or parents, would get up and leave. Would they find the messages of the piece too offensive?

Things seemed to go fine until nearly the end of the play, when I heard a disturbance and turned to see Kenneth and Gene, two young African American men, both self-identified as Christian fundamentalists, climbing noisily over classmates to get out. As they left the auditorium, I wanted to jump up and chase them back in, but that would have made even more of a scene. No teacher stopped them either. I knew that this wasn't an emergency bathroom break. Both young men were leaders in the school, well respected by many students. They were often eloquent about issues of social justice in the world, as well as issues of fairness at BAA. Kenneth planned to go to a Christian college to become a minister and then use his pulpit and art to bring spiritual healing to others. Gene had not yet decided on his career, but he was immersed in church music and accompanied a number of gospel groups.

After the show was over, some students told me how great it was and even thanked me for bringing Toscano. But other students, outraged, told me that they had seen Kenneth and Gene leave. "That's what we've been talking about, Ms. Nathan. That's just disrespect." They expected me to retaliate with disciplinary action. Our students are well aware of the code of discipline. It is an infraction to leave a required assembly or class.

As originally planned, Toscano spent the next day visiting classes, giving mini-acting workshops, and talking with students about the show and his acting career. Though my decision did not completely satisfy other students, rather than taking disciplinary action, I asked the two young men to meet alone with Toscano and discuss why they had walked out on his performance. I also called the parents of these two students to let them know that their sons had left without my permission. I expected that the young men would start an intense discussion of Christian theology and their own interpretations of biblical texts, and sure enough, throughout the day, I observed the students and Toscano in heated dialogue.

The young men quoted the passages from the Bible that they claimed condemned homosexuality. Toscano, his head tilted slightly to one side, listened respectfully. He offered alternate passages from the text that he felt embraced homosexuality. "But the point isn't for us to fight over who can quote scriptures better for our own arguments, is it?" His head tilted the other way, and his eyes held the two students. "It's really about whether we can tolerate our different opinions without dismissing one another." Toscano asked the students whether it was possible to move from tolerance to understanding. "That is why I perform this piece."

When Toscano finally left, I asked Gene and Kenneth what they thought. Kenneth answered first, "Well, he sure knows his Bible, but we just don't see things the same way." Gene added, "Still, it was fun watching how he develops his scenes. I got to give him props for knowing his craft. He sure is passionate about what he does."

I had wanted the conversations with Toscano to help them own their behavior—to admit that they had behaved disrespectfully by walking out on the performance. Deep down, I even wanted the dialogue with the actor to help my students consider the possibility of holding a wider perspective of tolerance and even understanding in their lives. This didn't happen.

I sat down with Gene's and Kenneth's parents, not without a certain amount of trepidation, and they eloquently defended their children's action. They quoted from the Bible to support their understanding of why this kind of assembly had been inappropriate in school. I tried to explain that the performer was also a Christian and that I felt that listening to the performance was not the same as agreeing with the message of the show. Gene's dad told me emphatically, "My son called me after he left the performance, and I told him that I gave him my approval to leave. I like a lot of what goes on in that school, Ms. Nathan, but this was just wrong. We should have had to sign a permission slip allowing our children to attend. This is against our religion." I tried to explain that we weren't trying to convert anyone to a certain belief system, but that our school rules demanded that students stay in authorized areas. Gene's dad came right back at me. He agreed with me in concept, but not in practice. I (and the school) had crossed a line and he backed up his child. I felt utterly defeated by this conversation. And I doubted myself. Maybe Gene's dad was right. Maybe we should have had permission slips. I wouldn't have even considered issuing permission slips for a performance addressing issues of race or language origin. I asked myself... so why should it be necessary with homophobia? I came out of my meeting unable to impose discipline on these students.

I consulted with other faculty about my inaction. Wouldn't other students see my lack of decisiveness as tacit approval for homophobia? How could we preach "diversity with respect" and ignore the students' actions? One colleague used my own metaphor and said, "You always say how we have to see things as half-full not half-empty. You should be satisfied that 98 percent of our students were willing to engage respectfully in the performance." I was and I wasn't. In truth, the whole incident made *me* too uncomfortable. In retrospect, I think the young men should have suffered more serious consequences for their rudeness and intolerance. But I didn't want to take on their parents and enter into this murky area of the rightness or wrongness of our values. So I did as little as possible. I took the low road. I'm not proud of my decision.

At the parent council meeting a week or so after the show, parents and caregivers expressed reactions ranging from gratitude for a sensitive portrayal of complex issues to disgust at the messages. Some parents hoped that we would also delve into other controversial issues, such as race and class. I never raised the walkout with our parent council, instead allowing the issue to be swept under the carpet.

Every adult at BAA wants our school to be a place where we can all engage in controversial discussions without checking out. And, most important, we want our school to be a safe place for all students. I believe that our commitment to our Shared Values will continue to embolden all of us—teachers, students, and parents—to push one another to engage, even when it makes us uncomfortable. I hope I can do better the next time I enter the uncharted waters of Shared Values. I can't help thinking about the possibility that we, by focusing on raising the achievement of our young men of color, unwittingly ignored the fact that sexual orientation might be a contributing factor to lack of success. Talking about race and achievement (which I will discuss in detail in a later chapter) is tough enough. How much tougher would it be to talk about homosexuality, when many members of our community see it as morally wrong, or a sickness? What about all the "invisible" gay or questioning kids? I could hardly expect them to talk about the ways that homophobia hurts them.

As school leaders, we all face the kind of dilemmas I faced with Kenneth and Gene. Maybe it won't be homophobia, but it will inevitably be something sensitive, something controversial. We have choices. First, we choose whether to ignore the issue or engage with it. There is no neutral reaction: ignoring is, I believe, tacit acceptance. Second, if we choose not to ignore it, we have choices about what to do when our actions bring down passionate disagreement, or even angry condemnations, on our heads. I believe that raising the questions and taking action is always better than ignoring. I know that I will often make mistakes when I take action. I'm not proud of the decision I made with Gene and Kenneth, but I am proud of the fact that when Mr. Mendes said, "Our students are thinking about this all the time, but we just do nothing," we asked ourselves hard questions and let those questions lead us to action. We didn't go on doing nothing.

WHAT CAN HAPPEN WHEN STUDENTS AND FACULTY JOIN FORCES TO SPEAK UP AGAINST VIOLATIONS OF SHARED VALUES?

The stolen alcohol incident

In the spring of 2005, some BAA music students performed at a local music club, as a fund-raiser for the music department. It was a wonderful concert; the house was packed, and family members and other supporters of the school watched the students perform brilliantly.

They were joined onstage by some of Boston's emerging professional musicians, who gave their time to support our students. However, the next day the owner of the club called to report that alcohol had been stolen from her establishment.

Ms. Torres gathered all the musicians together, and initially had an awful time getting any of the students to say they had seen anything. Finally, one of the young musicians, Martin, a leader in the band, said to the whole group, "Hey, listen, someone saw something. It will be terrible for our school and our reputation if we don't figure out who did it and make sure it doesn't happen again. Artists don't act like this. If you know who did this, you've got to say. I want to be back at the club next year. It matters for us that we play places like that. And they gave us the night for free. It'll get around town that BAA kids do this, and we won't be able to play anywhere. No one wants that." Martin spoke fervently, but still nobody talked, not for another few days. During these days, the entire school was buzzing with talk about expulsions and rumors that the music department would never be able to perform outside of the school again. In the meantime, Ms. Torres and security personnel managed to uncover the truth: which students had actually stolen the alcohol, which had looked away but knew what was going on, and which knew nothing because they hadn't even been in the vicinity. Finally, the culprits confessed. They were all suspended and the ringleader, Aixa, was expelled. This meant that she could not return to BAA. The family appealed the decision, and the hearings were endless. I never feel good about having to punish a student, but I always hope the student learns from punitive measures. I often question whether they do and whether I'm doing the right thing. But for all the anguish I felt about Aixa, when I look at what happened in terms of the well-being of the whole school, I see a lot of growth. This incident gave us a real opportunity to discuss "Community with Social Responsibility" as we pushed students to own their behavior.

Even though this incident only directly involved one group of students, so many students were talking about it that Ms. Torres decided to hold another whole school assembly. She also decided to have students talk to students rather than (as usually happens) expect administrators to chastise everyone. Ms. Torres asked Martin if he would address the student body and explain why this was such a big deal. She would talk about the repercussions from the incident— the suspensions and expulsions—without giving away explicit information about any one student. Ms. Torres explained, "I need you to talk about the larger issues, Martin. We need to resolve this. It is bad for the school and very bad for all of you." He agreed.

At the assembly, Martin got out of his seat, twirling his drumsticks in one hand. "We all know this school is pretty amazing," he began. "Sure, we've got beefs and there are things that we all think are stupid and try to change. Sometimes we do. I know all you freshmen want to have lunch off campus, for example. Well, maybe you can change that. But, you know, one thing that keeps us together is that we have these Shared Values. Sure, some of us might laugh when Ms. Torres gets on the intercom every morning telling us to live one of the Shared Values, but it's cool. We do believe in diversity with respect. Just look around at how many different kinds of people are in here. And passion with—" And then he held his mic out to the audience like a DJ as they responded, "Balance!"

"Yeah, that's right," Martin continued. "And we believe in community with—" And again the audience responded, "Responsibility."

"And, of course, also, wait a minute," Martin fumbled. "I don't know about that one. I never seem to get it right." Ms. Torres prompted him and he finished with, "Yeah, that, vision with integrity.

"So, like you've heard from Ms. Torres, they're dealing with the students who did this, but I just think we all have got to think about what this means for our whole community and our reputation out there. We live by our reputation as artists, and if it gets tight out there for us, we won't be performing, and that's not cool, you know what I mean?" For the most part, students listened quietly and respectfully to Martin. As everyone got up to leave, Ms. Torres, again, asked advisors to discuss the incident in advisory groups.

We didn't want students to dismiss the incident as "just something that happened to the music majors." Dumb, destructive behavior like this is common among adolescents. It would amaze me to meet a school leader who had never had to deal with theft, drinking, or drug use among his students. How many teenagers disrupt their proms by coming drunk or high? Sadly, it is just as common for students who witness the behavior to stay silent, or for the student body as a whole to react with a collective shrug or even laughter. As sad as I was that BAA students had stolen alcohol, and as disappointed as I was that other students hadn't turned them in, I was proud of our school's overall response to the incident. Martin's leadership meant so much to me. It established a norm that respected student leaders could support school values publicly without being seen as "ratting out" their peers or "sucking up" to adults.

STUDENTS OWNING SHARED VALUES: SOUL ELEMENT

And yet this was still a top-down education in values, led by and even enforced by adults. Here, as with Queer 101, it was a case of adults initiating the conversation and saying to students, "Let's think about Shared Values." We were very pleased, then, when soon after the music club incident, Martin and some of his friends met with Ms. Torres and me and asked if they could have their theater group, Soul Element, perform a new play for the school. The Soul Element project is a BAA group of young men of color who use drama to explore racial, gender, and social issues. The group has toured area schools as well as the country, and performed for national educational conferences. It not only addresses issues of how young men of color struggle to succeed in society, but also has become a support group for its own members. Participants encourage one another to stay in school and, most important, to do well.

Jason, who had been in the group since the beginning, spoke to us. "We perform outside of school, and we talk about all the issues in the school, but we've never performed at BAA. A while back we talked about the negative stuff that happens here, like this incident at the music club. But, we've got to talk about the positive things we do, too. Some of us do really care about school and want to do the right thing, you know, and we can show that onstage. We just want to perform here for our own peers." We agreed that the group would perform their new piece *Breaking the Stereo Types* at BAA as soon as it was ready, and that we would also hold student discussions after the show.

The play opens with Germaine, played by Jason, watching a video version of *Boyz n the Hood*. He's laughing and calling out to the TV, "Yeah, yeah, boy! That's one for you! You do it like that! Yeah!" His body moves to the rhythm of the rap music in the movie and his "yeah, yeahs" punctuate his approval and identification with "life in the 'hood." As the TV fades, the lights come up on Germaine, still swinging to the music we no longer hear, and cutting cocaine on the table. From the other room, his brother Lloyd calls out, "Come on, Germaine, we're gonna be late to school!" Lloyd struggles with his book bag, takes a swig of juice from the fridge, and yells again, "Germaine, I said we're gonna be late."

"I'm coming! I'm coming!" Germaine yells back. But the audience sees that he's not moving. He keeps cutting his cocaine and moving to that unheard beat from the music of the movie. Lloyd, impatient, crosses over to the room where Germaine continues to cut and move lines of cocaine. Shocked, he says, "What you doing? Mama's gonna kill you bringin' that stuff in the house! And we're gonna be late for school."

"Aw, go on with yourself. All you ever think about is school!"

"Yeah, I do think about school! I wanna be someone. Mama works too hard for you to be bringin' that stuff in here."

Germaine rudely interrupts his brother. "You think she don't know?! You think Mama don't know?! How you think we even pay the rent?! How you think we get those supplies for school? Huh? Mama knows. She done known for months now! You jus' got your head somewhere else, huh!"

Lloyd is too hurt and disgusted to say much but "Come on, we gotta go to school!" The lights fade as Lloyd grabs his book bag, and Germaine follows after putting his supplies away.

The play follows the complex lives and relationships of the two brothers as they struggle with the different choices each of them has made, and the choices that they each feel society has forced on them. The audience sees the brothers confronting peer pressure, teachers who don't care, violence in the community, and the importance, ultimately, of living a life that one can be proud of. It is a raw, deeply honest, and troubling portrayal of life in a poor urban neighborhood. It is also enormously hopeful. It speaks to the power of the individual to "do the right thing" even in the face of terrible choices, as well as the importance of creating shared responsibility for outcomes. The show doesn't preach, but it certainly gives the audience members ways to identify with BAA's Shared Values.

In a post-performance session for our students and an outside group of educators visiting the school, the performers were asked how they stay motivated to succeed. "Well, the play itself helps us," says Jason, the young man who plays Germaine. "Now, I was never really a Germaine, but I sure know a lot of Germaines." Lots of students in the audience begin to laugh. Jason went on to explain how his character was sucked in by the lure of easy money until he was too trapped to get out.

"Also, I've worked very hard to get on the honor roll. I didn't used to be, but I'm proud of it now." Students in the audience begin to hoot and holler, "You go, Jason!" "I used to make fun of kids on the honor roll. You know, call them names and everything. Not here I didn't do that, but in my other school. Now, when I hear that, like my little brother who's in middle school making fun, I say, 'Hey, quit it! It ain't even like that. It jus' ain't cool to get bad grades.'"

A teacher in the audience asks how the entire BAA community has "unpacked" the messages of this play. All the hands of the actors go up. Everyone wants to answer. The actors begin to speak.

"See, if you just fixate on Germaine's character then you're not really seeing the whole play," Michael, another student performer, says. "He's actually the only completely negative character. But he's caught and we want the audience to see that. We also want the audience to understand his brother, Lloyd, and Lloyd's determination to do what's right 'cause he understands the history of oppression of black people." Michael looks intently out at the audience and ends by saying, "We are taking you on a journey—through humor and really good character development—about how complex the African American experience is. I don't think we are preachy."

Malik, another performer, chimes in, "See, even though the target is African American people 'cause this play is specific to our experiences, it could be any group in a way. 'Cause what we're saying is not to judge until you know and not to give up 'cause you think it's easier. You go on this journey like Michael said, and the audience can identify with that journey and then maybe decide to make some changes."

Alex says, "I didn't used to be like Germaine, but I sure acted the fool in school, and then I got involved in this play. I knew it wasn't enough to just be a good actor. You gotta be a scholar, too. Like we say in our school—artist-scholar—and that's mad hard. I was so angry in tenth grade at my humanities teacher, Mr. Garcia, 'cause he just wouldn't get off my back. I hated doing homework. I always got yelled at, and then I couldn't pass the classes really 'cause I wasn't doing the work." Alex went on to describe how Mr. Garcia kept telling him just to take a risk and do some work and show it to him. He described how Mr. Garcia would start talking to him about passion with balance and how if he'd start some homework and finish it, things would get easier. "Then, one day, I did some of my homework and Garcia, Mr. Garcia that is, was really proud of me. Like he reacted differently to me all of a sudden. I kinda liked that. I did some homework again, just a little, and then things just started changing. But it was kind of like the way I train for a part in a play. You've got to keep practicing and repeating the same things and finding new things. You've got to be disciplined and focused, and then your scene work with the teacher and the class actually gets better. For me, theater is my training for life."

Soon students, like Alex, began to use the phrase "passion with balance" to talk about how to manage their time and the necessary multiple commitments to their arts and academic work. They now take the question of whether students are exhibiting "passion with balance" also to mean, Are kids handing in their assignments and staying healthy? Or am I being disciplined and focused? What began as an adult term has been embraced and expanded by the students. As time goes on, I imagine that all our Shared Values will take on additional meanings to each generation of BAA students.

HOW CAN SCHOOL LEADERS KEEP SHARED VALUES FRESH AND HELP STUDENTS OWN THEM?

In some respects the American high school is an unnatural construct. We adults put hundreds of adolescents together in one physical place and tell them they must pay attention early in the morning, when most of them would rather be asleep, in order to learn about different subjects. We go further and demand that these same adolescents follow a series of rules that we have created that are meant to keep them safe and progressing in ways that we have predetermined make sense. We expect them to understand what it means to be an American, how to participate in a democratic society, and why respecting others is important. Often, we also require our students to demonstrate that they know how to be socially responsible. We have rules, too, that prescribe those behaviors. This is not wrong. We are responding to society's expectations for our educational institutions.

But we can't stop here. Usually, the rules will initially be laid down by the administration—or sometimes the faculty—and students will either learn to toe the line or face the consequences. What I love about BAA is that while the faculty initially created our four Shared Values, we adults quickly realized that we had to find ways for the students to own and shape those values. Students must experience the values as their own—from the inside out. How else can schools be places that balance the structures (or rules) that adults know must be provided with student ownership and incorporation of those values represented by the rules? If students are not actively engaged as partners, if they don't feel that it is up to them to create a fair and reasonable community, why should they care about behaving in socially responsible ways? Why should they own their own learning processes if they can't own anything else about school? Many schools have active student governments, and this is certainly a way to engage students' voices, but it isn't enough. It is essential to create a common vocabulary that all students can articulate and return to as they monitor themselves and one another.

I need to remind myself that each year we need to reteach the meaning of our shared values. It's easy to forget that just because we spent a lot of time last year on "diversity with respect" that we don't need to this year. It can be exhausting for school leaders and teachers, but it is our work to keep these values out in front so they don't get stale. I continue to worry about how our students often don't treat each other or even the adults with graciousness or respect. Our students shut down easily when they are criticized. I wonder how we can really teach vision with integrity. Is integrity something you are born with, or can it be taught?

I'm proud we are a place where students can disagree. For instance, I allowed students to walk out of school when we first invaded Iraq. Sherry, a junior dance major, came to me, furious. "How dare you let students do this without giving others a chance to say that we agree with Bush's decision?" I was shocked. And then, I realized I had been so relieved that some students were politically minded enough to protest the insanity that I saw with the Iraq War that I had forgotten that my job is to teach, not preach. Sherry helped me organize a teach-in on the war that included all points of view. Next time, would I forbid the students to walk out? I don't know.

We have learned at BAA that without a set of tools like Habits of the Graduate, RICO, and our four Shared Values, which clearly describe our expectations about behavior and intellectual and artistic pursuits, it is difficult to increase student achievement. Having the tools doesn't mean that everything runs smoothly—far from it. However, these frameworks help us return again and again to the struggles and the significant social, emotional, and educational issues that our students face daily. Our shared values give us a way to confront vandalism like "white power," or a vehicle to discuss homophobia and even theft. The goal at BAA is to keep the language of Shared Values alive, fresh, and owned by students and teachers. That is a lot of work.

"Good morning, Boston Arts Academy! Congratulations to our Charlie Brown Blues Band, which just won second place in the High School International Jazz Festival. The time is now seven fifty-five, so please adjust your watches. Everyone should be in their classrooms. Remember to live the Shared Value 'passion with balance,' and have a good day." Every morning, I hear Ms. Torres, the assistant principal, reminding the BAA community to live one of the school's shared values. Students notice when she forgets. Teachers do, too.

Part II

Supporting Teachers

3.

Two Great Teachers

What makes great teachers possible, and how much can school leaders really ask of them?

What's wrong with this picture?

I've seen many images of teachers as heroes in American movies. From *Dangerous Minds* to *Dead Poets Society*, from *Stand and Deliver* to *Freedom Writers* to *Mr. Holland's Opus*, American teachers appear as voices crying in the wilderness, working against the odds, and dedicating themselves heart, soul, mind, and body to inspiring their students. Ask a class of aspiring teachers what kind of teachers they want to be, and, inevitably, they will describe the roles created by Michelle Pfeiffer, Robin Williams, and other actors.

It's interesting to me that almost without exception movie principals are hidebound, shortsighted, and bullying people who oppose the heroic teachers and should just get out of their way. Moreover, the teacher-versus-administrator paradigm also sets up great teachers as mavericks, working alone in their classrooms, creating a sort of "separate world" for their lucky students. The heroic teacher and her separate world shine even more brightly when placed against a background of mediocrity and small thinking in the larger school. That's an awfully seductive image, and many teachers try hard to create these "separate worlds." In the movies, heroic teachers devote themselves to their jobs so completely that they sacrifice their own wider lives in the process, and come to see themselves as personally responsible for "saving" their students. This model of teaching, I think, is terribly flawed and quite dangerous.

The message to principals like me, who see themselves as promoting and nurturing great teachers, is that "getting out of the way" is the best we can hope to do. In this chapter, I offer two portraits of great teachers at BAA, and ask what *allows* them to be great. I think this "allowing" is the real job of the principal, and it is far more complicated and difficult than "getting out of the way." In the previous two chapters, I have described a whole school framework of shared values and RICO—habits or attitudes to improve student learning. In this chapter and the next, I explore how we work just as hard to provide a framework for faculty, and our efforts to build a culture of cooperation among teachers—a paradigm in direct opposition to the "separate world" idea. I also ask how much, as a school leader, I can reasonably ask great teachers to do.

I'll begin by showing you two great teachers as they do their work at BAA. Although these two are different in personality and approach, they share key qualities that, for me, exemplify good teaching: *flexibility* and *strength*. Flexibility is the ability to use different techniques for different kind of learners; it is the skill of recognizing that each student is different and comes with a different set of instructions; it is the sensitivity to know that when a student doesn't understand what you are saying you don't talk louder and slower; it is having many arrows in your quiver, with the most important one being a sense of humor. Strength is related to flexibility. It is the ability to withstand the onslaught of twenty-six or more different opinions all in one class period, while recognizing that each student needs to understand the lesson—and often her own way. It is the ability to maintain high standards while challenging everyone. Moreover, strength is the ability to breathe calmly and grow taller and more stable while inside you feel like you want to scream or cry. And strength is the willingness not to get into a power play with a student to show that you are strong.

MS. CHAN'S WORLD

It is four in the afternoon. Most students have finished their regular classes for the day, but the hallways seem busier than usual. It is not uncommon for students to be at school from seven in the morning till six in the evening, but this level of hallway traffic seems excessive. "We have senior dance concert rehearsal," a junior explains as she zips down the hall, tugging on her leotard to make sure everything is in place. "Ms. Chan's just giving feedback on one of the pieces now."

"I hope she doesn't make Nikki cry," another junior comments as she follows her friend.

Ms. Chan, who stands only five feet tall on muscular bare feet, loves her students and wouldn't *want* to make them cry, but her bullhorn-like voice can sometimes do just that. And she doesn't mince words in a critique. She does, in fact, make Nikki cry.

"I don't think you've worked that hard on your piece, Nikki, since the last critique," Ms. Chan states. "The music motif is underdeveloped, and the piece doesn't meet the length requirement. The music doesn't work either. We already discussed that." Ms. Chan turns to the next dancer to continue the critique session. Nikki looks dejected and nods her head sullenly. She tries to hide her tears.

Another student, Siobhan, tries to comfort her. "You know how Ms. Chan gets. . . . She has a vision of where we'll all get to, and if we don't, she'll keep screaming till we do. You wait. Your piece is gonna rock. I'm in it!"

"How can you expand that phrase when you are onstage alone before the other dancers enter?" Ms. Chan asks Lauren, who stands before her panting as she finishes running her senior choreography piece. "Also, remember how the panelists suggested that you consider using music that might create the mood for the pain of memory loss rather than lyrics that express more literal ideas? Mary J. Blige's 'No More Drama' is just so obvious." Ms. Chan sits in a wide second position on the studio floor, her notebook in front of her between her beautifully arched feet. It occurs to me that in her body, as well as in words and practices, Ms. Chan models both flexibility and strength. What she says to Nikki and Lauren is hard. She is demonstrating her strength here, as a teacher who steadily pushes her students toward a high goal and refuses to let them slip down. But as she coaches Lauren, Ms. Chan uses what she knows about this student to guide what she says to her, demonstrating flexibility in speaking to individual learners.

Lauren nods, still breathless, not yet able to articulate her response. Ms. Chan continues, "Remember the piece we worked on about the separation of mothers and daughters to Mozart's cello concerto recorded by Yo-Yo Ma? That's what I'm talking about—music that enhances the mood rather than lyrics that tell a story."

"Yeah, yeah, that would be good," Lauren agrees, still catching her breath. "Or, what about that John Cage piece you introduced us to last year?" She looks at Ms. Chan for approval.

Ms. Chan smiles broadly and exclaims, "Oh that would be great! That would be such a different sound to work with." Ms. Chan's enthusiasm is infectious. I can see it written all over her face.

"I know what you mean," Lauren concurs. "That phrase you mentioned—the transition from dancing alone to the entrance of the other dancers who are like my shadow—that started off as a literal story about my grandfather's experience with Alzheimer's. I've tried to make it less about my grandfather and more about memory. That's what the panelists who came in to critique us suggested. I want to show how memories make up the person we are and will become in the future."

I smile myself, listening to this conversation going back and forth as Ms. Chan makes some particular suggestions for ways that Lauren can add to the phrase in discussion. "I want to see some more contact with the dynamics there," Ms. Chan advises. Other student dancers contribute different ideas. They are all completely focused. The performance is near and this piece means a lot to Lauren. What I notice is how Ms. Chan has been able to get Lauren to articulate her own ideas. So often, teachers resort to just telling a student what to do rather than helping a student figure it out herself.

Lauren goes on. "I'm really inspired by seeing the Martha Graham's *Diversion of Angels*. I'm not just interpreting my family's experience with Alzheimer's disease; I'm trying to show how memories play a big part in the disease."

"And your use of Graham's techniques works well for this piece," Ms. Chan adds. Lauren's face crinkles into a little smile. Shyly she asks, "Does that mean you like it?" Ms. Chan sees that Lauren is anxious for her approval and responds to that need (flexibility), while maintaining focus on an even higher level that Lauren can achieve (strength).

"It's coming along nicely," Ms. Chan concedes. "I see how you are working from Graham's artistic tradition to invent movements that are your own. Remember your last RICO review, Lauren?" Lauren leans forward, listening intently. "We talked then about taking risks and letting the work speak for itself. You have always been worried about what others would say or how I would react. That's a natural part of the process, but you can trust yourself more this year. Make sense?" Ms. Chan pauses.

"Yes, yes . . ." Lauren is still tentative, wary of what is coming next.

"You have refined your technique, and you are clearly grounded and confident with Graham," Ms. Chan continues. "Now, take some risks. Listen to your body. You can be inventive. You can fall off center. Experiment with new meanings of the forms. Let your choreography speak for itself."

"Okay," Lauren says quietly. She pulls on her heavy sweatshirt and gathers her belongings to change. Quickly, she goes to Ms. Chan and gives her a hug. "Thank you." Lauren rushes out. I think about Lauren's fear of "doing it wrong," and of displeasing her teacher. It is one of Ms. Chan's great qualities that she can address these fears directly and help Lauren learn to trust herself and take risks, even as she herself is a powerful presence who can inspire fear. Ms. Chan uses her own strength in service of her students' flourishing.

I don't believe that Ms. Chan is a miracle teacher, or that BAA is a miracle school. I don't expect Ms. Chan to do her work alone, or to make miracles happen for every kid. *All* schools and all teachers can help students create work that they care about as much as these students do. School leaders can't make it happen (would that we were so powerful!) but we can put structures in place that *allow* it to happen. For me, this means making decisions that put a huge priority on teachers having time—not only each day, but over multiple years—to work with individual kids. Even teachers who are highly skilled and committed, like Ms. Chan, need this precious resource in order to help students learn to let go of their fear, discover in themselves what they want to create, and then to develop the skills to do fine work. Just as dancers need to work their bodies every day to maintain flexibility and strength, so teachers need to "work out" with other teachers. Besides having time to work with students, I need to make sure that there is time for the adults to meet together and talk and plan with each other about their teaching. Left alone in a classroom, a strong, flexible teacher can lose strength (sometimes we have to put down the burden when it simply becomes too heavy for us) or lose flexibility as our "teaching muscles" get rigid and set in particular patterns.

Will Nikki be able to let go of her fear? How can Ms. Chan help her reverse a downward spiral in which small failures reinforce each other and failure itself becomes a self-fulfilling prophecy? Lauren's experience shows that as she succeeds, Ms. Chan is able to push her even further. When Ms. Chan urges her to take risks, Lauren can take that advice. The apprentice has learned to trust herself, as she sees that the master believes in her.

There goes a child who is learning, I think as I watch Lauren leave the studio. I'm awed, as I often am, by watching a master teacher at work. But I wonder: What about Nikki? Was her experience an important part of learning for her? I worry that Ms. Chan focused so much on teaching the Laurens of her class that she wasn't giving Nikki enough of her powerful attention. Is it right for me to expect Ms. Chan to be able to teach both Nikki and Lauren well? I think it is.

Her students see Ms. Chan as the epitome of an artist-scholar with tremendous currency in a world they want to enter. And, most important for high school students, they feel that they, too, are being taken seriously as artist-scholars. In some respects, they are Ms. Chan's colleagues. She will choreograph for them. She cares enough to bring other professionals to work with them. Even those who will never go on to dance professionally after high school know that a wider audience takes their work seriously. Of course, Ms. Chan's high expectations and brutal honesty, which to her are marks of respect, may make students like Nikki cry. As a principal, it is my job to continue to ask Ms. Chan the hard questions that will help her to reach all her students, even when she is tired and needs an extra push.

The kids we all see every day deserve to learn in school that their ideas matter. Ultimately, it is the teachers who communicate this to their students. When I think about resources, it is always teachers I am thinking about before anything else. They are precious, but they are not static "investments" or "assets." Great teachers are, fortunately for us, a renewable resource—but that means that principals have to make sure that they are renewed. Ms. Chan has made herself a great teacher—but it is my job to *allow* her to do her best work, understanding that she needs time, space, and support in order to do it.

Many great teachers crack or break after years of bearing the burdens of their jobs alone. Ms. Chan is an example of a teacher who, in body and mind, has remained strong, flexible, and happy in her work. I keep her in mind when I ask: What are the conditions that nurture her? How can I help younger teachers develop into the Ms. Chans of the future? And how can I make sure that I don't ever forget that Ms. Chan, too, needs continual support to maintain her vibrancy and flexibility?

I know that my ability to give helpful criticism is vital. I need to watch Ms. Chan teach and find the time to talk with her about my observations. I also strive to create structures that give her enough autonomy and authority to make decisions about teaching at the same time as I ensure that she has time to collaborate with colleagues. And finally, one of the most important things I can do—and by far the most costly and complicated—is to find time for Ms. Chan and others to be away from students in order to think, create, and be renewed artistically and intellectually.

As I watch kids like Lauren work with their teachers, I think about whether, and how, this arts-based model of master and apprentice, can work outside the arts classroom. In our school we try to draw inspiration from the arts for our academic teaching and intellectual enrichment from the academic courses for our arts teaching. As the principal of an arts-focused school, it is particularly important for me to guard against the arts classrooms at BAA becoming the "special worlds," and arts teachers, through their very success, allowing students to believe that the rest of their classes are somehow ordinary, less magical, less important.

It may seem easy for Ms. Chan to create the master-apprentice relationship that I have written about here, since students come to her predisposed to learn dance. They come into her studio hungry to learn what she has to teach. They don't have to be dragged in the door. Fewer students come into a mandatory math or English class with the same hunger. How can a teacher of a required academic subject, looking at a room studded with reluctant or downright hostile learners, seduce these kids into the kind of passionate commitment to the subject that Lauren demonstrates?

Students often come into our school excited about their arts studies, but prepared to be bored by academic classes, even expecting to fail them. One common refrain at BAA is, "I hate math. I never did well." So how can academic teachers engage students in content that may be difficult, boring, and foreign to them while remaining attuned to and aware of who the students are? Students come into classrooms with a history, a prior relationship with the subject. If that relationship has been bitter, sour, or traumatic—if struggling with reading, for example, has left scars of failure or humiliation on a young person's spirit—how can a good teacher help them heal? Mr. Ali gives us a glimpse of how this is done.

MR. ALI'S WORLD

Mr. Ali's senior humanities class has just begun. The radiators bang loudly in an intermittent and disruptive rhythm, emitting perhaps too much heat for the cramped room. In such a small space the twenty students feel like fifty. Two teachers' desks, bookshelves, and a metal closet are jammed into the back corners, and students, a paraprofessional, and a sign language interpreter have to squeeze into the chairs crowded around the pushed together tables. When students get up to move into groups, they have to step over and around chairs, book bags, and one another, making sure not to pull the computer wires from the extension cords.

The walls are covered with posters, artwork, student work, baby pictures of students for an autobiography project, and hand signs on a poster for an American Sign Language class that meets there as well. Hung high on one wall is a quote from Paulo Freire's *Pedagogy of the Oppressed*:

"There is no such thing as a neutral education process. Education either functions as an instrument that is used to facilitate [the integration of] the younger generation into the logic of the present system and bring conformity to it, or it becomes the practice of freedom."

This humanities class includes black, Latino, white, and Asian students. One student is in a wheelchair and works with the paraprofessional, while another student is hard of hearing and needs the sign language interpreter. Some of the students participate in "open honors," a school-wide program that allows them to earn honors credit while remaining in the mixed-level class. Others will work hard to reach the minimum college-prep benchmarks. The class is purposefully mixed, both by arts major and by academic skill level.

Mr. Ali is a founding faculty member at BAA. He has helped to develop the four-year humanities sequence at BAA, which he calls a "many-headed hydra" because it is a combination of language arts (English), social studies, history, philosophy, and economics. The humanities curriculum focuses on the development of critical thinking and reading skills as well as oral and written expression. While BAA has paid attention to city and state content standards, this curriculum reflects BAA's mission to integrate arts and academics, and create "engaged members of a democratic society."

Humanities teachers, like all academic teachers at BAA, teach two courses per semester within their discipline, with an average student load of about forty-five students per semester. With writing seminar and advisory, teachers are responsible for approximately sixty-five students per semester. In most other urban schools, teachers will teach approximately one hundred and fifty students a day. At BAA most academic teachers only have one preparation a day, for example ninth-grade humanities or twelfth-grade science. Almost always, therefore, teachers will meet the students as either freshmen or sophomores and then again as juniors and seniors. Part of my job as a leader is to fight hard to maintain this kind of manageable "load" for teachers. This is part of what allows Mr. Ali to do the great work he does. To make this possible, however, Mr. Ali has to be willing and able to teach a huge range of content, rather than sticking to the traditional content areas of English, social studies, art history, and so on. He must become flexible in his knowledge of content, as well as in his approach to individual kids. It's a lot to ask of one teacher.

Dressed in his usual wonderful and somewhat wild attire, with a colorful tie that stands out from a striped shirt with a bright white collar, Mr. Ali stands before his senior class on the first day of the semester. He was born in Uganda to Somali parents, lived in Saudi Arabia, studied in India, and at age thirteen came to Boston, where he was raised by an African American pastor considered by many to be an icon in his community.

Mr. Ali begins class, welcoming the group he already knows well, and mapping out the work they will do in this last, most difficult year of their humanities class. Some students are completely engaged and attentive; others furiously draw in sketchbooks; some students perk up a bit at the sound of Mr. Ali's voice. Aleysha, a large-boned young woman, her hair in tight cornrows, sits shrouded in a puffy winter coat, her head and body turned away from Mr. Ali as if to say, "I'm not listening to you," as she furiously picks at her cuticles.

Sounding almost like the narrator on *Survivor*, Mr. Ali describes the challenges ahead, speaking to students by name. "Carolyn is a dancer, but she will be challenged this semester to leave her comfort zone of dance and embrace the understanding of other arts disciplines. Similarly, Joshua and I need to approach the materials as more than humanitarians. We love the humanities but we will need to leave our safe places, and approach these materials with different aesthetics. That won't be easy for us. Maybe easier for Joshua because he is visual artist. But, what do I really know about dance?" Mr. Ali's inclusion of himself as a student seems to make Joshua grow taller and sit prouder. At the same time, Aleysha turns even farther away from Mr. Ali and becomes even more preoccupied with her finger-nails. He seems not to notice the perpetual scowl on her face or her posture of rejection. At least he says nothing of it at this moment.

He continues, "Remember our essential questions for this course: Why do we bother with art? What attitudes do we or should we have about art? How can we learn to locate the aesthetic of art? We will start by reading Aristotle's *Poetics*. Aristotle, the great Greek philoso-pher, who you will learn much more about, grappled with these same questions."

Later in the class, Mr. Ali directs the students' attention to their first assignment, to closely read the text by Aristotle and prepare questions for the class discussion. "As you look over the rubric, what are the areas that you would say you aren't very comfortable with right now?" he asks. "Where do you need to improve? Where do you know you have trouble? What will challenge you?"

Hands shoot up around the room. Alan speaks first. "I know that I have a hard time changing my mind and really actively listening like it says here on the rubric. I have strong opinions and I usually agree with myself. I ignore people if I don't agree with them." There are some titters around the room.

"Yeah, I feel like that, too," Aleysha says suddenly, whipping her head up and leaving her cuticles alone. She glares at her classmates and speaks with a challenging tone. She is an alto in the chorus and has a lovely melodic singing voice, but her speaking voice is usually loud and angry. "I can get really aggressive if I disagree with people. It's hard for me if I get heated. And I can get heated. I also will shut down if the environment gets hostile and I don't feel safe." This last phrase is said almost as a threat to the class that they not get "hostile" with her.

"Yes, you can shut down," Mr. Ali agrees. "And it's my job to keep the classroom safe for everyone. This material matters to you a lot,

Aleysha. I know that. Your writing and participation in Hum 3 last semester really showed it." In the calm way he has just addressed her, Mr. Ali has confirmed Aleysha's "smartness." It is subtle, but brilliant. This young, seemingly angry and disengaged young woman cannot restrain her smile. And when she smiles, her whole being lights up, and she is truly beautiful. As I watch her, I imagine what is going on in Aleysha's head. She knows that Mr. Ali respects her thinking, and her writing. I see her remembering that they have had a four-year relationship, starting with freshman year humanities. He has proven to her many times that he is fair. She knows he makes her work hard. Mr. Ali is demonstrating the flexibility that I see in so many great teachers. He is certainly strong in his expectations and standards (like Ms. Chan), but he is also a master of adaptation, stretching and reaching in an effort to engage every kid in his classroom.

Aleysha, I expect, remembers how many times Mr. Ali forced her to refine and revise her Humanities 3 paper until she finally got a 3.3 on a 4-point rubric. (All students must achieve a 3, which is a proficient rating on the ten-page persuasive essay. Without a 3, students repeat the class. There is no summer school class for Humanities 3.) Her claxon tones from the previous year echoed down the corridor as she cheered, "I passed my Hum 3 paper! Yes, I did. I got a 3.3! I'm gonna be a senior!" She high-fived anyone she passed. "Look! Look!" She held her paper aloft like a trophy, shoving it in anyone's face within range. The freshmen looked at her like she'd lost her mind, and nodded at her, fearful that the paper or Aleysha might somehow do them bodily harm, but Aleysha didn't care. She had achieved a major milestone at BAA and she was proud. It was Mr. Ali's strength that allowed him to maintain high standards through what I'm sure was a painful struggle with Aleysha and her drafts. It's so easy, as a teacher, to give up after the second or third effort: to say, without really meaning it, "That's good enough."

More than anything, at this moment in class, Aleysha knows that

Mr. Ali respects her. She may have momentarily forgotten all that on this first day of the semester since she hasn't been his student for a few months, but this exchange refreshes her memory. She shifts back imperceptibly into the center of the classroom and the conversation. She has forgotten her cuticles. She is now visibly present.

"And for you, Jameson?" Jimmie looks up. He had seemed to be dozing, but he is ready to respond. To everyone else in the school Jameson is Jimmie, but Mr. Ali uses his "proper" name, and this seems to help Jimmie realize that his active presence in class matters. Maybe it's like wearing dress clothes; you don't act out as easily. The formality of his name brings a seriousness of purpose to the discussion.

"For me it's hard to come prepared. I want to, but I have too much going on. I know I need to focus better on school if I'm gonna graduate. I want to come prepared. I do. But I sometimes don't do the reading like I should."

Mr. Ali nods at Jimmie's comments. "Thank you, Jameson. I appreciate your honesty. I truly expect this seminar to be a different experience for you. I know it can be." Jameson nods somewhat sheepishly. In ninth grade he was brilliant in class discussions about issues of race in America. He eloquently challenged his classmates about why he would never use the n-word even though it's part of popular culture today. He told his classmates about the history of the word.

Looking at Jameson, I think about what an exceptional student he is. Over the years, however, he has spent too many painful, sometimes angry hours in my office. I have had to suspend him for drug use; bring his aunt in because he was not making the necessary grade point average to stay in his arts major and thus the school (he's a musician); and watch him spin out of control. He wants desperately to stay in the school, but the lure of the street and easy money is strong. His best friend has been arrested for drug possession and for weapons. I question whether Aristotle and aesthetics will be enough to hold him in school. This is when I wonder about teachers and limits: I know that it's not up to Mr. Ali to save Jameson. Mr. Ali knows this, too, at least rationally. But if he takes responsibility for Jameson, even unconsciously, eventually he will burn out. What can I do as a principal to guard against this? How much is too much—and how much is not enough?

"If you can't focus in class, Jameson, it is acceptable to get up quietly and go to the bathroom and take a brief walk. That is considered polite. It is impolite to fall asleep in class or to shut one's eyes."

"I just have a hard time like the paper says moving the conversation forward," Joshua, a tall African American visual arts major, concedes. "I like to argue and I always think I'm right. Sometimes, like you say"—Joshua looks at Mr. Ali—"I argue just 'cause I want to and I'm not listening." Mr. Ali breaks out into a smile with that last comment.

"I didn't have to say it! Thank you, Joshua." Mr. Ali says, demonstrating his flexibility again. Joshua and Aleysha have owned their challenges (using RICO without mentioning it). Mr. Ali has rewarded them for their honesty, rather than punishing them for failure. "So"—he turns to the whole class—"this isn't easy. You see the ways in which you have to prepare for seminar. Now, you need to read the assigned text and write at least one question."

Mr. Ali moves the students into groups, and they carefully climb over tabletops and chairs, trying not to create too much chaos. In groups of three or four they will practice the methodology by discussing an excerpt from the text they have just read. Mr. Ali explains that for this day, he has chosen the passage from the text, but normally, they would be responsible for choosing the excerpts for discussion.

Jameson is paired with Ellen and two other students. Ellen has a one-to-one paraprofessional who works with her since she reads on a significantly lower grade level than any of the other students. Nevertheless, after discussion, she is able to participate, and no one seems irritated to work with her. The groups are fairly random in terms of ability level or prior knowledge, and all students seem comfortable with their assigned partners.

Aleysha is working with Katy-Ann, a slim, quiet ballet dancer. Katy-Ann's blond hair is still done up in a ballet bun since she had dance class this morning, and no time after class to take her hair out. They make an incongruous pair. Katy-Ann is from a middle-class family and her dream is to attend a conservatory, like Juilliard, to pursue her career as a ballet dancer. She came to BAA from a small private school because of the dance curriculum, and moreover she wanted to finally attend a public school in her community. Katy-Ann rarely gets off-track and is consistently on the honor roll.

Aleysha is twice Katy-Ann's size in height and in weight, and is known for having one of the loudest voices in the school. She is looking at community colleges with some resentment because she had wished to attend a conservatory, but she just can't afford it. (The Boston Conservatory, one of our partner schools, does not have enough funds for students who are good, like Aleysha, but not superb.) Aleysha lives with an aunt and cousin because her mother died of AIDS two years ago. Both girls read well, but Aleysha is easily distracted by her friends. She is barely passing math, not because she can't do the work, but because there are always friends to attend to instead of homework.

"Stop that, Michael," she hisses at one of her friends across the room. "Can't you see we're doing the questions?!"

Mr. Ali approaches Aleysha's table, blocking her view of Michael. "This reading should be really interesting to you," he says. "In fact, we touched on some of these questions in Hum 3, but not in depth. Here's your chance to really dig in, analyze, argue, defend your position, give evidence. Give it to us! I know you can do it!"

Although Mr. Ali speaks to the class, Aleysha senses the personal challenge and cheerleading directed at her. She knows he knows that she can do this reading, and do it well. And, as she looks at Katy-Ann studiously bent over the reading, she seems to soften for a minute, perhaps thinking that it isn't fair to Katy-Ann to distract her.

"Come on," Aleysha urges, "I'll read this section and you read the other, and then we'll jigsaw it like we did in Garcia's class."

Jigsawing is a technique students learned in Mr. Garcia's humanities section during the first part of the semester. I am happy to notice Aleysha using a skill she learned from one teacher in order to do a task for another—one example of how teachers support each other's work. The object of jigsawing is not to read an entire article oneself, but to concentrate on one section in-depth, and then share that with the other members of your group. Thus, everyone becomes expert in one area, learns from one another, and then can absorb and comprehend the entire text.

"That way we both won't have to read the whole article," Aleysha tells Katy-Ann, who seems relieved to have Aleysha on task.

Their heads bow down over their readings. Everyone in class seems focused.

The interaction I saw between Mr. Ali and Aleysha is not the result of magic. Mr. Ali comes into his classroom with some crucial advantages. He knows his students well—socioculturally and personally. He understands how to hook his students academically through their passions in the arts. He values and respects his students as artist-scholars, because he has seen their work and talked with them about it. He works hard to use language that his colleagues, who are arts teachers, have used. Finally, he collaborates with his colleagues. He is not a lone, maverick teacher, but a member of a team. This means that he doesn't carry the entire burden of planning a curriculum, teaching it, and assessing student work on his own shoulders. Instead, he works with this team that helps him think through the very best way to do the job they are *all* doing.

Aleysha comes in the door with some invisible advantages, too.

If she was facing a teacher she didn't know, and who didn't know her, Aleysha's boldness might have come off as the rudeness and attitude of another "sassy African American teenager." This hypothetical teacher, seeing Aleysha primarily as a "type," might have felt she needed to "come down on that attitude right away." Of course, few teachers would ever speak openly about Aleysha's race, but many high school students who look and sound like Aleysha have dropped out and been lost to the school system. At BAA, she has been given an opportunity to develop a trusting relationship with a teacher who is with her for the long haul. Aleysha has another advantage, too. During her day, she will probably struggle with boredom and defensiveness in some of her classes. But she will also sing with her peers, work in an ensemble, study theory and piano, and prepare to perform in front of friends, family members, and many younger students as she tours in the elementary and middle schools. Her confidence soars in her music classes, and she is still learning to transfer that joy into her academic classes.

Success truly begets success. (The opposite is usually true, too.) This plays out in Ms. Chan's class, but we see it even more clearly in Mr. Ali's, where students are not all here by choice. Mr. Ali can build on Aleysha's engaged identity as an artist to encourage in her an engaged identity as a scholar. He has listened to her concerts over the years, and he knows she has a gift and love for music. It is his challenge to create the same set of expectations and joys in his own humanities classroom. So Mr. Ali reaches out to Aleysha without embarrassing her. While blocking her interaction with Michael, he did not engage in a power struggle, but deftly reminded her, through his whole-class reminder, that she is a competent, educated, and capable young woman. He allows Aleysha to feel both safe and respected by her peers. Like Ms. Chan, Mr. Ali remains both strong and flexible.

It is not easy to teach Katy-Ann, Aleysha, Jameson, Joshua, and Ellen in the same class. Each student is at a different academic level, and each comes from a different sociocultural and economic background. Even though Mr. Ali knows a great deal about each student's background, and has also thought deeply about and practiced many different techniques as he strives to be successful with such a heterogeneous class, he meets with varying degrees of success each day. Sometimes he feels like he is not giving students like Katy-Ann enough of a challenge. He worries that Jameson has missed a lot of school days and may not graduate at all. He feels frustrated that no matter how hard he works with Ellen, she seems to retain information for only a couple of days at a time. And his deaf student has not noticeably improved in her English writing, even with the help of the deaf education teacher. And what about Aleysha? Will her success at BAA be enough to carry her forward into college? Has she developed enough stamina to sustain her through higher education?

These questions plague Mr. Ali. Has he been successful in teaching his students that it's the sustained effort—the marathon—that will enable success in the long run? A sprint is much easier, and that is always his students' fallback plan. Stay up all night and finish the assignment, but don't really spend the time necessary. That is too hard. These endless questions and worries make Mr. Ali's job extremely demanding. He hopes that in the final count, successes will outweigh frustrations and failures with students. But sometimes, and some days, the whole endeavor can seem pretty grim. As his principal, it is my job to help him know when to say "that's enough," to preserve his own strength for the ultramarathon that a teaching career can be. I do that by finding the time to talk through how he is feeling about a particular class or student. I hope I can help him regain his perspective when he's discouraged. I remind him about students with whom he has been successful. "You never thought you'd get through to Kyle. You did." I also try to help by reminding him that tomorrow is another day and that his own family needs him now. "The work will be here when you come back. Get some distance now."

SO HOW CAN A SCHOOL LEADER HELP GREAT TEACHERS
STAY GREAT? AND HOW CAN WE HELP THEM SET LIMITS
ON THEIR TERRIBLY DEMANDING JOBS?

Like many teachers, I began my career alone in the classroom, with
the door shut, and developed my skills alone. Many of my colleagues
began this way, too, and the structure of the schools they work in
does not encourage or expect them to open it again until retirement.
I was trained to think about teaching as a singular pursuit, devoid of
collaboration. I think I was also trained to think about teaching as
a kind of missionary work: to be a good teacher meant to be a hero.
But, in my training, there were no teams of heroes. To become a good
school leader, I had to learn to question everything I thought I knew
about the nature of teaching.

Teaching at BAA is decidedly not a solitary activity. While I have
very little influence on what goes on moment-to-moment in Ms.
Chan's or Mr. Ali's classroom, I can, and do, work on the schedule
(the skeletal system of a school) to ensure that teachers help each
other, that worries and questions are shared among team members
and the entire faculty. Mr. Ali meets weekly with academic and arts
colleagues to discuss students and to develop curriculum. At the end
of the year, he will spend two days with his team reviewing and critiquing each other's units and lessons, and creating notebooks on the
year's courses so that they continue to build a collective archive of
work.

Mr. Ali and his colleagues are good teachers, and as a principal
I know how lucky I am to work with them. But more important
than their individual gifts is their ability to function as a collaborative team—the humanities team. These teachers have debated,
compromised, selected, rejected, retooled, rethought, researched,
and reflected again in order to write the best possible twelfth-grade
curriculum. They have brought in teachers from other disciplines,

particularly arts teachers, to complement or assess their curriculum designs. They have learned to accept criticism, to be willing to admit to needing help, and to work in partnership. They have invited academics from other fields, such as local professors of economics, to broaden their content knowledge. Arts teachers go through similar processes in their disciplines by inviting outsiders in for critiques and to sit in on team meetings.

Mr. Ali and Ms. Chan are not "one-offs" or "the exceptions" at BAA. I tell their stories here as representative of the ways in which our teachers can be successful. As a leader, it is my job to build a school in which all teachers work in teams, and have the time built into their schedules to talk, to visit each other's classrooms, and to create curricula as carefully and self-critically as artists create their pieces. If I do my job well, teachers will develop relationships with each other and with their students that are strong enough to withstand the enormous, sometimes crushing, pressures that the world puts on all of us.

At BAA, teachers work purposefully together to evaluate all of the seniors, not just their own students, on individual and group projects. Just as the students must collaborate, so must the teachers. Learning to be vulnerable with one another is as important for teachers as it is for students. In Humanities 4, students spend each term with a different teacher and synthesize their knowledge from both sections at the end of the semester. One term Aleysha will be with Mr. Garcia, the next term she will be with Mr. Ali. Her grade will be a combination of both terms, as well as of two teachers' feedback. Both of her teachers will grade her work. It is a complex system that requires teachers to agree on content and assessment tools, and to communicate clearly about student progress. Teacher-to-teacher accountability is required and practiced. It is not just Mr. Ali who holds the key to Aleysha's success: the entire team is responsible. The same occurs in arts departments, where the entire team will judge a senior's exit requirement or participate in a jury. In this way, although each teacher must be strong and maintain standards in his or her own classroom, the team can take on some of that "hard" strength, so that the individual doesn't break under the strain of student resistance.

Teachers need not all be from the same background as their students, but BAA does require that everyone embrace students' varying backgrounds as fundamental building blocks for developing both curriculum and student-teacher relationships. Mr. Ali and Ms. Chan understand this intuitively. Other teachers need to work harder and require the collaboration and assistance of their colleagues to ensure that they are always open to the many ways of understanding their students. Teachers help each other maintain flexibility by stretching each other, challenging each other to look at a student or a task in a different way. Teachers are also vital in helping each other set boundaries. When Mr. Ali worries out loud about Jameson, another teacher is likely to tell him gently, "We're all working to help him. And, ultimately, we must accept that there are limits to what we can do." I like it when I hear one teacher tell another, "Time to go home now."

Even as districts and states feed schools a more and more poisonous and limited diet of teacher-proof curricula, Ms. Chan's goal, and the goal of her colleagues, is to work intensely in collaborative teams to figure out the best ways to reach our students in order to bring them to high levels of achievement. The teachers I work with at BAA, like Mr. Ali, don't use the fact that students' skill levels are too disparate or that there is too much violence or poverty in their neighborhoods to justify failure. This isn't because they are saints (although I frequently find them to be incredibly admirable), but because this kind of blaming would take too much time away from the "good part" of their job, which is tackling challenges together. We all struggle continually to figure out how to do our part of the work, hard as it is, so that our students can take their places on the world stage.

4.

Teachers Talking Together

What are the risks and rewards of transforming a faculty into a professional learning community?

Last year I interviewed a prospective teacher, Jocelyn Bernard, for a science position. Jocelyn had taught for a year in another urban school system and had used the same engineering curriculum we were implementing. I was excited that Jocelyn had also worked as an engineer for a number of years, and that she was a young woman of color. But as the interview progressed, I was dismayed by the experiences she reported to us about her first year of teaching. Sadly, I felt that in her all-important first year she hadn't learned requisite teaching skills and that she would be joining us with lots of baggage to get rid of.

In her school Jocelyn had taught more than one hundred and fifty students a day, and although she benefited from a coach who visited her classroom every two weeks or so, no mentor teacher had been available to her. She was assigned to teach a science class that had a number of special education "behavioral students" in it, even though she had only taken one summer school class in special education. By law Jocelyn was supposed to have had a special education teacher co-teach this class with her, but this teacher was usually occupied with the testing of the special education students.

Jocelyn shared some of her successes and challenges with the engineering curriculum. "The resource kits never arrived at my school, and so every night I developed all the experiments myself from the textbook." She told us that she spent literally thousands of dollars of her own money purchasing materials.

"What about professional development?" Ms. Bautista, one of the BAA teachers on the interview team, asked her. She looked at us quizzically. Ms. Bautista expanded. "When did faculty meet together to plan curriculum? Did faculty observe one another teach?"

"Well, yes, we, the ninth-grade team, did meet together, almost every day," Jocelyn explained. "But we didn't plan curriculum or talk about lessons. There was never time for that. We had to talk about attendance and tardiness, since it was such a problem. There were always lots of forms to fill out since the administration was trying to get extra funds from central office to help with truancy. Also, we spent meeting time analyzing the quarterly city-wide tests and the state standardized tests, too. We had the scores from last year's ninth-graders to go over—"

"I don't get it," Ms. Bautista interrupted. "You weren't looking at the scores of your current students?"

"Well, we didn't have those scores at the beginning of the year, so we looked at standardized tests in English, math, and science from the previous year to see how to improve our teaching."

Then, we learned from Jocelyn, when the test scores came in for the current students, teachers would carefully analyze which items students did poorly on and map those back to the standards that the district expected them to have taught. The premise was that this would help teachers figure out ways to "improve" their teaching. The idea of analysis leading to improvement is well-intentioned in theory, but in practice it had created a kind of stifling "got you" system that created anything but good results. Although Jocelyn's students had not done well on the science test, they had done better than students in the other high schools in her district. Her administrator had congratulated her, but the scores for the rest of the district were abysmal. Jocelyn couldn't feel good about that. She told us, "There is just never time for an opportunity to talk about teaching since the analysis of test items is so time consuming."

During the term, a literacy coach had met with the whole ninth-grade team and reviewed strategies for incorporating literacy into all the content areas. While Jocelyn found the ideas very interesting, she didn't feel that she was yet familiar enough with her own curriculum to think about an additional strand, and she worried that since no one ever observed her teaching literacy in her engineering curriculum, she wasn't doing a good job. "The goal was for all of us to teach a literacy block, but that never happened, so we're just supposed to add it on to our primary content area. It's been a pretty overwhelming year. I guess I'm just looking for a school where I will get more support and where teachers actually talk about teaching instead of just about test results and forms that have to be submitted to another office."

When I heard this committed, creative young teacher talk in ways that suggested she was already burning out in a job she should have loved, what stood out to me was something that may not have been in any way obvious to her. Understandably, she was focused on herself. The system precluded anything else because of the relentless demands of her job. I, on the other hand, heard the underlying story of the failure of a professional learning community.

On the surface, Jocelyn was doing what school leaders ask all teachers to do: teach content in engaging ways to her students so that they could learn. Schools teach students, after all.

But the schools that work best and encourage teachers to do their best work—as BAA does, I would argue—are more than "content factories." They are what some educators call "professional learning communities." I embrace this concept, even if it can sound a little jargony, as a profound and powerful ideal. A professional learning community exists in a school when the entire faculty and staff, including administration, works together toward a shared set of standards and assessments that are known to everyone, including the students.

Such a school is a learning environment not only for the students, but for all the adults. No one ever feels that they have "got it right," that no more learning as a teacher is necessary. Teachers continue to examine the standards they have taught, and they retool assessments as students become more proficient. Teachers and principals know that in a professional learning community there is continual growth, risk-taking, and trust among and between everyone—teachers, administrators, and students. Certainly teachers have opportunities to learn content, but how and in what conditions they learn both individually and together, how they share their practices, and even how they disagree is what constitutes a vibrant learning community. No one rests on their laurels. Everyone supports one another. Critique is not something just for students but for adults, too.

Of course this is an enormous undertaking. In already established schools, there may be resistance to teacher buy-in. Still it is worth all the efforts since in the end students will benefit.

MS. MILLER'S STORY: A MATH TEACHER LEARNS
FROM HER COLLEAGUES AND HER STUDENTS

Early one fall, I met with Ms. Miller, a beginning math teacher at BAA, to check in with her about how she felt her classes were going. Ms. Miller had done her student teaching with us, and I had hired her happily when we had an opening. Everyone on the math team thought she was perfect for our school. Unlike Jocelyn who, sadly, had been damaged by the failure of her previous school's leadership when I met her, Ms. Miller had been "grown" at BAA.

"I don't know," she began, tentatively. "I don't seem to ever be able do enough for my students. It's so much harder than last year." Ms. Miller had been a confident, even ebullient, student teacher. She took everything in stride, even being tired. Now she seemed more fatigued and worried than I'd seen her before. "I didn't think it would be so different. I know so many of the kids. But maybe it's not having another teacher always there in the classroom and to always bounce ideas off of... I never go home before six or seven p.m. because there is so much to do. I'm either correcting assignments, planning lessons, contacting parents, or meeting with individual students after school. I guess I'm pretty overwhelmed."

I understood that overwhelmed feeling. In fact, Ms. Miller's story brought me back to my own early years teaching math—I might well have said some of these exact same things. I know the time involved in correcting papers, planning, and contacting parents and kids. I also notice that it's the teachers who will be the best in a few years who are hardest on themselves in their first year: they see such a gap between what they *want* to do and what they *can* do. The young teachers who think they are doing fine are the ones I truly worry about. I could talk about some strategies with Ms. Miller, but now I wanted to focus on how she felt about classroom management. I'd observed her first-period class a few times and knew she wasn't happy with her students' lack of engagement. I smiled, leaned toward her, and said, "Tell me how your first period is going." I always try to show teachers who work for me that I am there to help, not judge, them. Of course I must give them negative feedback at times, but if teachers view their principal as a scary "teaching cop," their instincts are to conceal or deny their problems. At BAA, it's very important that we reveal these problems to each other.

"It's really hard," Ms. Miller went on, sounding a little more sure of herself. "You know how I believe that students should work in groups for projects. I think that is such an important way to learn math. But this class is resisting it. My second period—it's like night and day. They come in, form groups, and get down to business, but the first period... I don't know. They have no enthusiasm. Maybe it's because it is first thing in the morning...I even had some of these kids last year with Mr. Lonergan, but that doesn't seem to help."

"Can you give me an example of what happens?" I asked.

"Absolutely," Ms. Miller said. "Here's one day: I'm just finishing writing the 'Do Now' on the board, and Laura, you know the junior dancer, starts with: 'Just give us the worksheets, Miss. I don't want to be bothered working with Ian and Michaela.'" Ms. Miller and I laugh a little at her dead-on impersonation. I know Laura, and I can just picture her giving Ms. Miller attitude like this every day.

"In response," Ms. Miller says, picking up the story, "I insist: 'The point is to work on these problems together. You will be describing your work to the rest of the class in a group, too. I am interested in how you solve problems together, not just that you get the answer.' I mean, if I was a student in my class I'd think this was more interesting than worksheets...but the class is dead, and resistant on top of that. Next week, it's my turn to present a teaching dilemma at math team meeting. I'm ready. I have plenty!"

"That's great. I'll join you in that discussion. I bet some good ideas emerge."

When Ms. Miller brought her disappointments about her first period class to her math team meeting, Mr. Lonergan, Ms. Baez, Mr. Gaynor, and the student teachers on the team all listened to her, ready to help brainstorm solutions or just to discuss frustrations. Some suggested that she had to be stricter with the first period class. Mr. Lonergan, who had taught some of the students before, said, "Some of those kids are used to getting away with stuff—especially Laura. I had her two years ago. She's a strong student, and she doesn't ever like to slow down to explain anything to anyone. But she does want to get good grades. You have to remind her that this is part of her grade." Ms. Baez suggested that she watch some of the kids in their arts class. "They are mostly dancers, right?"

Ms. Miller liked the idea of watching Ms. Chan's dance class. I thought it was a great idea, too. "You're right, many of my students take Ms. Chan's modern class, and Ms. Chan and I are professional development partners anyway, so I need to watch her teach. This would be a great reason! I want to see how Laura behaves there."

At a subsequent meeting, Ms. Miller described her awe as she had watched her distracted math students excel in their modern dance classes. "First of all, Laura is the leader. She is right there in the front row in the middle. She is super awake and she gets the combinations faster than anyone, sort of like how quickly she solves equations in math." Ms. Miller snapped her fingers for emphasis and went on.

"Ms. Chan explained to me that sometimes she puts Laura in a group with students who are as skilled as she is, and sometimes the groups are more mixed. The other interesting thing is that Ian and Michaela are in that same class, too. But Laura isn't impatient with them there, even though they aren't as good technically. They're in a dance that Laura is choreographing, and she seems to appreciate their expressiveness and willingness to take risks. The whole feeling is different from math class." Ms. Miller reported her observations energetically.

Ms. Miller shared her observations of how the dance class started with a set warm-up; then the students worked on some center floor routines; then, they did across-the-floor work. The last part of class is more group work. She wondered if she should make her math class much more predictable. Aloud she mused, "Almost set it up like dance class, and don't start with the group work."

She went on to consider how she could implement a similar structure in which students start individually and quite independently, and then she would introduce a new concept and then finally move to group work. "Maybe I won't get quite as much group time, but I think I'll have a more engaged class. Ms. Chan is coming in to visit my class next week. I'm sure we'll have other ideas after that, too." There was a real hopefulness in her tone that had been missing from the previous week's meeting.

"We also talked about ways to think about graphing functions through movement. I would love to see how I might connect some of the algebra that we are working on with the choreography projects Ms. Chan is beginning. That got me thinking about where the process of choreography is like learning mathematics."

The level of trust that BAA has worked hard to create among colleagues is responsible for Ms. Miller's ultimate success with her students. Ms. Miller understood that she could admit to needing help without fear of negative repercussions from her administration or peers. Most team meetings are structured so that teachers can bring teaching dilemmas to the table. Teachers feed and support one another, both within and between disciplines. Teachers ask questions such as, "What can I do better to help my students become more successful mathematicians? Is there anything in the arts, or another discipline, that will help guide me?" We have made it a priority to have time during the school day to talk and think critically together about teaching and student success. Once a week, students come later in the morning so that teachers can meet in small groups, and another day, students leave earlier so that the full faculty can meet together. Ms. Miller's professional development partner, Ms. Chan, works with her as a coach and mentor, but not as an evaluator. After Ms. Miller visited Ms. Chan, Ms. Chan visited her classroom. "I'd move Laura up front," Ms. Chan suggested. "Let her feel like the leader." Mr. Lonergan also visited Ms. Miller and made some suggestions about pacing.

At BAA, teachers have access to at least two or three different views of the school. This is purposeful. Ms. Miller, for example, is a dance advisor as well as a math teacher and an instructor for the tenth-grade writing seminar team. A few weeks after the discussion in the math team meeting, Ms. Miller had the opportunity to participate in a dance class herself—an event that truly changed her students' view of her and hers of them. She reported back to me what happened. "I couldn't believe how energetic and creative Laura is. And my other students, too. You know what Gina said to me the next day in class? 'Hey, Ms. Miller, you're so willing to learn in our class, we gotta be better in your class.' Now those were sweet words!" Ms. Miller smiled broadly.

MY STORY: LEARNING ABOUT PROFESSIONAL LEARNING COMMUNITIES BY BUILDING THEM

I was fortunate enough to live through the genesis of a professional learning community at Fenway High School from the school's beginnings in the mid-1980s, and I brought those experiences with me to BAA. Larry Myatt introduced us to the concept and set up the schedule so that we could meet as a team. He modeled the importance of listening to students as well as adults, always with respect. At Fenway, we developed a core foundational course, Social Issues, which all teachers taught, no matter their primary content area. We agreed early on that we would all teach the same units more or less at the same pace, and that we would implement many engaging large and small group activities. We agreed to bring all of our two hundred students together regularly in the cafeteria to read together, and we invited guest speakers.

Social Issues was our shared endeavor. We planned and discussed both the content of the classes and how we would approach these controversial issues—in other words, we had to discuss our teaching with each other. We also had to evaluate our students together, since we shared the same unit tests—and this meant that we were essentially critiquing one another. If one teacher's students did uniformly well, we would ask: what did that teacher do to ensure such success with student learning? Conversely, we expressed concern if another teacher was less successful. This is by far the more difficult skill, of course. Mr. Myatt's signature sense of humor helped us practice it. Teachers are very sensitive about their work and very nervous about "stepping on toes." We had to learn to be honest with each other and to drop our defenses. We had to figure out how to support each other so that all our students were learning the material at more or less the same level of proficiency. Over time, Social Issues became the way we defined our professional learning community, and it became our entry into talking about a range of issues in our school.

We all taught the class at the same time—first period—and all students took it. Fifty percent of the curriculum focused on issues such as the civil rights movement, busing in Boston, the war in El Salvador, and nuclear proliferation. The other 50 percent, designed by students, dealt with issues of adolescent development such as violence, sexuality, music, or friendship. Since the topics engaged our students, we offered the class first period as a way to "hook" them into arriving at school on time (we had a terrible tardiness problem). Our strategy worked pretty well and attendance increased. Students didn't want to miss the discussions, especially those that dealt directly with "their" issues.

We had to agree on how we would present content, such as the notorious school desegregation case in Boston, which was still very raw for many families and teachers. And we needed to be very thoughtful and strategic about lessons related to HIV/AIDS, since this was in the mid-1980s when the epidemic was just beginning. We were a very diverse group of teachers from many different religious, social class, and racial backgrounds, and it wasn't easy to construct common units and the accompanying assessments that we could all do together. Although we only had two forty-minute periods a week to plan the curriculum and assessments, many of us stayed late in the afternoon to ensure that our lessons were well-crafted. Furthermore, we knew we needed the time together to talk about how our students were faring.

A professional learning community needs nurturing and leadership. At Fenway I was in charge of the development of the Social Issues curriculum. This meant that I prepared materials for the rest of the team to critique and adapt at our weekly meetings. I also volunteered to be videotaped teaching a lesson. (Even though teachers generally enjoy being up in front of our students, being videotaped is usually an excruciating experience. Many of us are videotaped when we are student teachers and vow to never, ever let it happen again!) I would be ahead of the others so that they could critique my lesson first, before teaching it themselves. I felt nervous at first being the "guinea pig," but if I was willing to put myself out there, it would make it easier for everyone else to be vulnerable in this way. Eventually, other teachers offered to have their lessons videotaped.

The majority of students in all ten Social Issues classes performed similarly on unit assessments. But there was one class where the students always did poorly. The closeness the faculty had developed by working together on Social Issues and the systems for sharing information and observing each other helped us figure out why.

We noticed that this teacher, Mr. Donnelley, who had been assigned to the school and who was nearing the end of his career, regularly missed school days during horse-racing season. He owned a racetrack and many horses, and essentially, it turned out, had two jobs. Although he always had doctors' notes excusing his absences, they were very disruptive for students and for the school, needless to say. His Social Issues class was often left without a teacher, and the students were angry since they had become invested in the topics. We tried to make do with substitute teachers, but that was not a reliable solution. Sometimes I would merge his class with mine, but it was difficult to have a sustained conversation with fifty students in the room. We tried to talk with Mr. Donnelley about ways to improve his attendance. We wanted him to understand how his behavior was eroding our professional learning community and the students' fledgling sense of community as well as their achievement. His students were the least prepared for the end-of-unit exams and the least engaged in the curriculum, since their classroom discussions were so erratic.

I talked to a couple of teachers about a somewhat radical idea. What if we asked his student teacher to take over his class and the school to provide the student teacher with a stipend? (I had a small grant to support the curriculum development for Social Issues and asked the grant maker if we could divert the money this way.) Although this would mean that none of the teachers would receive a stipend to continue our after-school planning work, when I brought the idea to the entire team, all the teachers preferred working voluntarily in order to ensure that all students had their own consistent teacher. It was more of a hardship for us to have an unprepared substitute teacher, or to combine two classes, than to forego the extra money.

It is surely possible that in another situation, teachers would never agree to this kind of intervention. But in our context at that specific time and place in our school's history, it seemed like the best decision. I was pleased that we could all acknowledge what a drain and a strain it was on the rest of us and on the students. It was my job to talk to the absentee teacher, and I was a bit worried about it. Would he be offended? Embarrassed? To my surprise, he didn't seem particularly bothered by the decision. From his perspective, it wasn't really his problem that he was out so much. He couldn't help it, he said. And, he had the doctors' notes to prove it.

At Fenway, I was very fortunate to have colleagues who decided with me that we did not have to allow an external situation that seemed beyond our control to destroy either our community or our students' achievements. The professional learning community provided a structure that both revealed a problem that might have lain undiscovered at another school, and at the same time provided the path to a solution.

So many principals have encountered similar situations. The question is always: what can you do? Sometimes you *cannot* do what you know is best for students and even for other teachers. Sometimes you just have to wait the situation out. Sometimes you cannot rock the boat. While there are many reasons why our intervention might not have worked at another school, it also rarely works to be victimized or to assume that something is beyond your control. Often, those of us in leadership positions feel we have to figure everything out by ourselves. Sometimes we cannot share personnel issues with others, but I am glad I made the decision to talk to my colleagues about the absentee teacher; otherwise, I'm not sure we would have collectively made any decision that helped kids.

BUILDING A PROFESSIONAL LEARNING
COMMUNITY AT BAA

When I had the chance to open BAA, I wanted everyone to teach a core class as we had done at Fenway. In the spring before BAA officially opened with students, I held a series of meetings with a range of participants—artists, academics, community members, parents, college students. I asked the same question at each meeting: what should BAA graduates know and be able to do? I felt that by asking a generative question such as this I would both garner community support and involvement for the school and I would, of course, hear good ideas. Although a range of answers always surfaced, there was always one common response. "BAA graduates had to know how to write a grant. Artists live and die by grants." That was our motivation to begin our school-wide approach to writing. Teaching writing would be the foundation of our own professional learning community.

We decided that all teachers would coteach writing seminar, and all students would take it, and at the same time of the day. This would be our core course. Co-teaching would create a natural pairing for professional development partners. Teachers would observe one another in writing class and then also in the teacher's primary subject area. Seminar became the place to develop and practice a school-wide approach to teaching and assessment.

Anne Clark, our curriculum coordinator, helped us create our grade level writing seminar class, which became the central place for professional development. When I hired Anne we agreed that she would be our first teacher leader. I know how important it is to have many teacher leaders on a faculty, and my job has always been to ensure that I am providing enough opportunities for teachers to grow as leaders. In defining Anne's role, I suggested that she should teach a class herself as she worked to guide other teachers. I knew her role was particularly important for our emerging professional learning community, and that teachers needed to see her as a teacher first. She was, and is, an excellent teacher. She was our resident literacy "expert," and knew all the current educational literature about how to improve students' literacy skills. Her job was to plan lessons with and for teachers; watch teachers teach and then give critical feedback; and teach a particular lesson or skill that a teacher felt unsure about how to introduce. She was always open and eager to have teachers critique her as well.

Ms. Clark also helped us wrestle with teacher accountability. She convened and led discussions about seminar so we could create a school-wide rubric (or list of criteria) for judging good writing, and also connect that rubric to our Habits of the Graduate and RICO. Anne provided examples of good student writing so that we could agree on what constituted proficient writing. By scoring student writing individually as teachers, as co-teaching pairs, and finally as grade-level teams, we developed shared teacher accountability.

Accountability has now become a buzz word in the education reform literature, where it is often code for judging teachers, principals, and schools based on test scores. For us, it means being accountable to each other in the ways in which we assess student work. We had to learn to question why one teacher could give a student a very high grade on the writing rubric while another did not. If a teaching pair didn't share similar views on what constituted good writing, that wasn't fair to students. We spent many hours collaboratively grading work and then discussing why we had given a certain grade. Over time, we would reach consensus. Ms. Torres and I taught seminar in the early years, and we struggled along with the teachers, leaning as they did on Ms. Clark's expert assistance. It was important that we, too, could admit frustration and failure.

I always looked forward to those faculty meetings (which, by the way, is a radical statement; most teachers and principals look forward to faculty meetings as much they look forward to root canal work), because I loved seeing how we would come to consensus. Sometimes, in the beginning, we needed Anne's help. She could always be the "outside expert," and deferring to her judgment felt natural. Now, I'm happy to say, the teams are pretty independent.

Here's an example of how this collaborative work actually happens: Morgaen and I team-taught ninth-grade seminar. We each read one of our student's autobiographies—an early assignment. We discussed our grading process and our scores. She had given the student a 2.5 (out of a possible 4.0 points); I had given her a 3.0, because I felt that her use of descriptive language was very strong. After a brief discussion, I agreed that I had been, perhaps, too generous. Then, we met with Ligia and Paul, two other teachers reading the same ninth-grade student's assignment. They had both given the student 4.0. We were surprised that our scores were so far apart. We listened to their reasoning. They, too, felt she had strong descriptive language, but also that she used a strong voice and had well-developed paragraphs.

We disagreed. The four of us went back and forth and eventually called Anne over to help settle our dispute. Anne explained why she felt that the paper was not a 4.0 but closer to a 2.8 or even a 3.0. We agreed on a 3.0 after a lengthy discussion. Now, for anyone used to the traditional way of grading, this could look like a disastrous waste of time. If it had been me grading alone, I would have given the paper a 3.0 after perhaps fifteen or twenty minutes of consideration. Instead, four people spent well over an hour in order to arrive at the same conclusion!

But the four of us saw it differently. We all learned a lot from the exercise. Our disagreements had been healthy and primed us to look more specifically for real evidence of descriptive language. We also discussed in more detail what a well-developed paragraph looks like. The following month when we did the same activity with a different assignment, the four of us scored the piece almost identically. Among the four of us, none of us were certified English teachers. Morgaen, as a history teacher, had the most experience with writing. Ligia, a world language teacher, had an excellent grasp of writing in Spanish and, Paul, a music teacher, had never really assigned or graded written work before like this.

Our original premise, which I think still holds true, was that it is less threatening for teachers to develop a set of shared expectations and practices for a course that everyone teaches but that is no one's primary content area. Very few of us were writing experts. What mattered for our students' success was that we all grew to share an understanding of what constituted good work in writing and how to teach the necessary skills. For me (and I think I'm typical of many teachers), the idea of scoring work with others was initially intimidating. I was nervous when I first shared my scores with Morgaen. What if she thought I was too soft? Or too hard? What if I thought that of her? I had to get beyond the fear in order to trust my colleagues—that no one would belittle anyone else, but that we would also work together to understand why a teacher gave a particular score, and then we would argue with evidence if we felt that our score was the correct one. We all committed to the process and to consensus. In this way, we all grew as teachers and colleagues.

Because of this intense working together for writing seminar, we learned to transfer these skills to other content areas. Paul, Ligia, and Morgaen all began to develop department-wide rubrics in their content areas and everyone practiced scoring work together.

Now that we had a structure around which to build our professional community, we could explore what that community could do. We found that it allowed us to do several distinct things: as well as developing a shared accountability system, we could diagnose our students' weaknesses, as well as the gaps in our own teaching; we learned to critique one another's practice; and we found ways to get to know our students beyond the classroom.

TAKING RISKS

Ms. Jong sat slumped and exhausted in Ms. Torres's office. "I just feel like nothing I do is right. I can't get through to Ashley. I'm not sure I can get through to Janet either." Her face was crestfallen. Her shoulders were hunched and she looked like she carried too much pain for her twenty-five years. Ms. Jong's despair reverberates with that of many young idealistic teachers who try and teach a great lesson and fail. What was different in this case is how Ms. Torres, her administrator, handled it.

Both girls had been suspended because, following Ms. Jong's science class experiment with cell phones and what materials might block a cell phone signal, a brawl had broken out after school. Earlier in the day, Ms. Jong had participated in Janet's suspension hearing. "I didn't think for a minute that the activity would lead to so much drama. When Jeff [a security officer] came to me and explained that he had both girls in separate Student Support team offices because they had gone at it after class, I was just shocked."

Jeff had told Ms. Jong that since BAA doesn't allow the use of cell phones in school, the class had been an opportunity to see whose numbers each one had on her call lists, and sure enough, both lists included Angel and that caused suspicion, and then a whole he said-she said thing, which turned into a fight. Ms. Jong had heard something in class about Ashley explaining to Janet why she had Angel's number, but she didn't think anything about it. She was just excited that everyone was engaged in the experiment using tinfoil.

"I didn't realize it would cause such controversy and eruptions later. I feel so terrible. This was really my fault." She sighed dispiritedly.

"Maybe I just don't know how to connect with this population. I didn't grow up with any of the pressures that Ashley or Janet has." She explained that she would have probably been thrown out of her house if she'd ever even thought of hitting another kid in school or anywhere else. "Play an instrument, respect the teacher, do well in school, go to college—the values of a stereotypical Asian family. Maybe I just don't understand Janet and Ashley. I sometimes wonder if I'm what they need as a teacher. They may have beautiful voices, but how will they ever do in college? They haven't even turned in any lab reports. They are failing my class!"

Ms. Torres listened and calmed Ms. Jong down. "You are the right teacher for our kids, Emily. You are an excellent teacher. You are incredibly creative. You know your content. Now, maybe I wouldn't have used cell phones as an experiment, given that we say kids can't have their cell phones visible in school, but you couldn't have known that they would fight. Sure, maybe you should have been more attuned to the culture of that class, and the tensions brewing, but you did your best. That is the most we can all ask from ourselves." Then she outlined the plan of action to address the violation of "community with social responsibility": first, a mediation for the girls when they come back from suspension; second, a behavioral contract; and finally, a letter of apology. "It's not okay to interrupt the learning of others. Ever. They are both on the Student Support team's radar as kids we need to watch. We know that there are lots of other issues going on with both of them individually. I can't even get a parent up here for Ashley's hearing."

Ms. Jong despaired. "I'm just embarrassed that I can't control my own class."

Ms. Torres responded firmly. "You can. This was a difficult situation. You are still learning about classroom management. I'll bring Janet back into class on Friday, and see that everything goes smoothly. A Student Support team member will also stop by every day through the end of the week. This isn't for you to solve alone. That's why I'm here, and Student Support, and even Ms. Montes, Janet's advisor. This is something we all will work on together."

It is distressing that in many schools, teachers like Ms. Jong would never feel comfortable enough going to their administrator for help, but Ms. Jong and Ms. Torres cotaught writing seminar together the previous year, and Ms. Jong has also seen Ms. Torres struggle to reach a student. Whatever the reasons for the lack of support in many schools, too often the Ashleys and Janets end up right back in the classroom after a brief suspension, with little progress having been made to resolve the disagreements with each other that brought about the suspension.

When I was a new teacher and had a discipline problem like this, the last person I wanted to go to was my principal. I would have been too worried about being judged as "bad." In the too few after-school meetings or professional development days we had, the principal and assistants just barked out statements about how to maintain appropriate behavior in our classrooms and the importance of discipline, almost at all costs. If there was any professional learning community, it was on the sidelines and just with a few teachers who came together to support one another individually.

Ms. Torres may not have agreed with Ms. Jong's choice of a lesson for her students, but she certainly doesn't blame Ms. Jong for trying a new idea. She may question Ms. Jong's judgment, and wish that she had consulted with her or others on her team about her "innovative lesson," but Ms. Torres is committed to creating a culture in which teaching practices are seen as continuing endeavors in improvement. If teachers (and students) don't feel encouraged to try new techniques or assignments, readings, or lab experiments that might not work the first time, why would teachers or students, or parents for that matter, ever trust that they had a stake or responsibility in the outcomes of any decisions?

Ms. Jong is a new teacher who has learned that taking risks and being vulnerable about her practice is accepted and expected. Veteran teachers like Ms. Clark, Mr. Ali, or Ms. Chan are also willing to make mistakes and share their challenges with their peers. The strength of Boston Arts Academy is that no matter how seasoned a teacher you are, everyone is always learning. That is what risk-taking is about—pushing one's own learning to another level and being willing to try something different that just might be terrifically successful—or not. As Ms. Jong has said, "Part of what makes risk-taking possible is knowing that your colleagues and administration will 'have your back,' that you will not be out in the cold, left to figure out both lesson planning and classroom management on your own."

Asking for help began as an expectation in writing seminar at BAA; this expectation then permeated the rest of our teaching practices. None of us were experts. None of us could do it alone. We had to keep asking one another, in meeting after meeting, were we sharing our worries and frustrations and still making plans for tomorrow? How does a school leader create the environment for that delicate balance?

Still, not every teacher is as willing and open to sharing as Ms. Jong was. Mr. Nichols, a music teacher at BAA, found little use for a professional learning community. He and Ms. Clark cotaught writing seminar and worked together on the eleventh-grade team. They planned together and graded together, but Ms. Clark continued to feel that she was carrying the fuller load. She asked me to read some of his comments on his students' concert reviews, and I was disappointed that he gave so little feedback. He certainly could get his students in his jazz ensemble to sound great together, but he assigned very little work that involved writing, analysis, or even composition. His passion was for performance. Whenever I complimented him after a concert, his response would be something like, "You see it takes a lot of practice to put on something like that. We can't spend all our time on written work!"

Both Ms. Clark and I tried to explain that it wasn't an either-or. We just felt that his students would benefit from some more rigor in the curriculum. Yes, performance was important, but so was reflection and learning to critique someone else's concert, and a well-developed music vocabulary. Even after the entire music department developed a clear assessment rubric for all students to use when reviewing a concert, Mr. Nichols's students did rather perfunctory work. I began to think that Mr. Nichols's resistance had to do with his own fears of writing. Even though we were a "writing school," as the students liked to say, we couldn't get Mr. Nichols to participate.

A professional learning community that embraces everyone, such as we have struggled to create at BAA, can be a lifeline for veteran and beginning teachers, administrators, students, and even parents. But what do you do, as with the case of Mr. Nichols, when it's not making much of a difference? Mr. Nichols was a tenured teacher, and short of eliminating his job, there really wasn't much I could do. At Ms. Clark's urging, I finally met again with him and explained that we had worked on these issues for almost a year and that I would now have to move into an evaluative mode. I knew he had received only good evaluations in his career and that this would be devastating to him. "I know you are a good music teacher. I know you have always been a good music teacher. But what I need you to do here is much more than you have ever done before. I feel that BAA has given you all sorts of supports to grow and change, but I don't see you excited or willing to try anything new." I had the painful job of explaining that neither did his teammates or colleagues.

Fortunately for BAA, Mr. Nichols resigned at the end of the year. He is now the head of a music department in a large comprehensive high school, and he has a show choir that is the darling of the school. I often hear comments about how great his choir is. I'm glad for him. I'm glad it worked elsewhere and that we didn't get into a protracted battle. Usually the choices aren't easy for principals. Do you ignore a less than excellent teacher hoping he'll leave? Do you turn up the heat, as I did, hoping that he'll change? And, if he doesn't change, and doesn't leave, what then? The answers to these questions are as complicated as each individual teacher.

One of my colleagues often tells me that if she only had one or two Mr. Nicholses, she'd do what I did: turn up the heat. But she has too many. For some, she just has to wait for them to retire. She doesn't have enough administrative personnel even to deal with all the Mr. Nicholses in her school. Her first priority is to create an administrative team that understands how to support teachers to become better. At the same time, my colleague is overrun by student altercations. She has too many students in her school to deal with each case carefully and thoughtfully; there is not enough student support or administrative personnel to provide helpful interventions; there are too few alternatives for students who need a different kind of classroom environment. She has young teachers, too, like Ms. Jong, but she can only sporadically provide support for them. She knows that this is partially why good teachers, like her, leave the profession prematurely. There just isn't the time, money, or resources to create a vibrant professional learning community.

CONCLUSION

Each year we refine our school-wide goals. These are the underpinnings of our professional learning community. Unlike typical district mandates that might change given the political winds, BAA's goals have consistently focused on our efforts to increase student achievement across racial, gender, and socioeconomic backgrounds. The vocabulary we use may shift from year to year, but the intentions have remained the same since we opened our doors—improved student achievement, and access to quality higher education and professional careers. Our entire professional learning community concentrates on these school-wide goals. Teachers write individual professional development plans using them. Before teachers do their peer observations, they review one another's professional development plans and try to connect their observations to the areas in which their partner wants to improve. Even students and parents/caregivers discuss these goals. Including them in the dialogue about how to increase student achievement can ensure that all constituents feel part of a school's professional learning community.

Schools often get derailed in their pursuit of increased student achievement and the advancement of a professional learning community because the buy-in on the part of all teachers is lacking. My colleagues in other schools talk about their disappointments at the ways in which small groups of teachers can filibuster to such an extent that decisions or action steps that would improve achievement for the majority of students never occur. Just the other day, a principal colleague described how his faculty nearly voted in a new schedule that would have provided time for an advisory block and a weekly planning period for it. He had led the faculty in discussions all year about the benefits of an advisory program. Teachers had visited other schools with advisory; they had read articles; students had been enthusiastic as well as parents. Teachers had genuinely understood the importance of personalized attention (advisory) for each student in order to increase student success in school. However, a small group of teachers managed to create enough dissension and discomfort within the whole faculty that they eroded the faith of the majority of the faculty and the proposed schedule lost by one vote. It's intensely frustrating to almost have a majority and then lose a key vote, but it is something we all must reckon with. How can we keep the faith that next time the good idea will be voted on? This was the threat we faced at Fenway in the early stages of the school's development when we had to deal with the horse-owning teacher whose negative behavior nearly toppled all of our work. We worked creatively and hard to figure out a way to marginalize his impact on our students. In retrospect, I think the time we had spent really growing the professional learning community played a crucial part in our success.

School leaders can consider multiple strategies that increase trust among teachers. School-wide courses and experiences, taught by all teachers, offer one way to build a professional learning community. It doesn't have to be a writing or Social Issues course. Many schools are now broken into small learning communities (SLC), many of which are organized around particular themes such as media, technology, or health. The intention of SLC is that by breaking down the size of a school, and giving it a unifying focus, there will be more opportunities for teachers to share a common curriculum, meet together to discuss similar projects, and align their assessments. The prevailing notion is that small is better because teaching (and thus learning) will be more personalized for students. I don't believe that small by itself is a panacea, although certainly it is important to reduce the number of students that any one teacher works with in the course of a day and week. Again, simply offering an array of courses in a particular field, no matter how relevant to students' experiences, doesn't create a professional learning community. How can small learning communities go further and institute a core course that is taken by all students and taught and discussed by all faculty? In my experience, improvements in student achievement might then be more evident. I have witnessed the positive results of inclusive core courses at both Fenway and BAA. I offer a core course as a possible solution, but the key is for every school to find its own solution for how teachers can effectively create and sustain a professional learning community.

How can school leaders and teachers keep the weight of the logistics of just "doing school" at bay and keep asking the hard questions necessary for the creation and survival of a professional learning community? There is so much pressure from school districts to respond to the demands of standardized test data and to improve student scores by "any means necessary." Many schools provide time for teachers to see which questions students got wrong on a variety of standardized tests, but the time to ask *why* students made those errors is never sufficient. *Why* questions are usually more complicated, more nuanced, and the answers may require developing different strategies to reach those students. Too often we succumb to time pressure and just deal with the *what* questions. But if we are committed to raising student achievement, pushing ourselves to keep asking better and more complex questions is essential to a healthy school.

Part III

Addressing Inequality

5.

How Do We Talk about Race?

How are discussions of race and achievement taken on by a healthy professional learning community?

Mr. Wilton squeezed his tall, lanky frame into a chair. "I really appreciate this time with both of you," he began as he settled in at the table in my office. "In my old school, we were really on our own. Let me show you why I'm so upset." He spread his grade keepers across the table in front of Ms. Torres and me. "There are the first term grades for my ninth-grade physics class." He had grouped the grades by race and gender.

All of his students who had received As were white. Even the majority of his students with Bs were white. Most of the students receiving Ds or Fs were African American or Latino boys. There was a smattering of students in the middle with Cs, but the vast majority of his students had received either honors grades or a failing grade.

Mr. Wilton's shoulders slumped. He was completely demoralized by these racially lopsided results. "I know these kids! I could *be* Kenny or Andre or Delvin. I live around the corner from Andre. I get the struggles they are dealing with." Mr. Wilton had left teaching in the suburbs because he wanted to work with students like Kenny and Delvin, but he worried that he was, perhaps, too removed from today's youth culture. "Failure was just not an option in my house growing up, no matter how poor we were," he said. "All I know is I can't stand to see another young man of color fail.

"I just can't figure out what I've been doing wrong," Mr. Wilton went on, his voice anguished. "I've always mixed up the students in groups across race and gender and social class. I have them doing experiments and activities, real hands-on stuff. Just a week or so ago, Andre presented his group's experiments to the entire class and did a superb job. I was really impressed. He had honors grades on projects and class work."

Mr. Wilton described his horror when those who did well on the final exam were mostly the white students. He felt that he had been very clear from the beginning of the term that the final counted for 40 percent of the grade. He had distributed study sheets and held voluntary study sessions after school. He had explained, more than once, that to get an honors grade in the class, you had to get a B- or better on the final—even if you had honors grades on classroom, homework, labs, and projects. The whole science team had talked about this assessment breakdown and everyone was in agreement.

"But now, it's as though my kids didn't even hear me. Or at any rate, they didn't know what to do with what they heard. How do I accept these outcomes? We've got to do something about this!"

I listened to Mr. Wilton carefully. I knew he was a committed and inventive teacher. I had watched him engage his students; they knew not to mess around in his classroom. I'd heard him say time and time again, "Learn to learn. Let's not waste a minute of time here!" Students stretched to meet the high standards he always set. But the spread of the grades he showed us was not unusual; it mirrored results in many classes at BAA. I wanted Mr. Wilton to know that he wasn't alone in his frustration and that we would bring the power of our professional learning community to bear on this problem.

"You are right that this situation isn't acceptable. It makes us all furious. It should," Ms. Torres began. "What makes it worse is that we keep seeing these kinds of results. One of the fundamental reasons for starting BAA was to find different ways to narrow this achievement gap. That's what we are here to do. But we know it's tough going."

The fact that at BAA white kids were succeeding at higher levels than black or Latino kids began long before they walked through our doors. Our data were beginning to show that the BAA students from more middle-class backgrounds in Boston tend to be white and have attended better schools (often private and parochial schools) and have better math, reading, and study skills than our students from poorer families. They aren't necessarily smarter, but they've probably had more skilled teachers. They haven't been taught by the year-long, poorly qualified substitutes who are assigned to classes in many of Boston's middle schools. Most of our students from Boston schools have been in classes with as many as twenty-eight or thirty students, often with only one teacher who is just beginning her career and with no assistant teacher. The large class sizes, substandard facilities, and outdated materials at these schools all contribute to lower achievement. Nonetheless, we were determined to do more than bemoan the problem, blame it on earlier schools or other factors beyond our control, and go on: we challenged ourselves to do more *here and now.*

Before we could begin to tackle this school-wide problem, the teachers and administrators needed more information than one classroom could give us. First, a group of us charted each student's record over his or her entire school career. As I looked at the numbers and charts I had to stop myself from feeling as demoralized as Mr. Wilton had first felt. What were the larger questions the data showed? What *didn't* the data tell us? One teacher on the subcommittee said, "Even our honor roll is distorted by race and gender. We have to say this aloud and say it to kids. Not in a blame-shame-attack way, but to acknowledge the situation together." I agreed. We also had to show the data to parents. We needed everyone on board as allies.

I told the faculty, "Together we need to learn to talk about race and class and to link those discussions to changes in our practice. I know having those conversations will be really difficult, but we need to focus directly on where we struggle most."

What is the achievement gap, really?

There is no more talked-about issue in American education, and no more agonizing one, than the achievement gap. For the majority of educators of good will who are teaching in urban schools—many of them, though obviously not all, white women—the achievement gap is a hugely personal issue. The notion that today's schools are not helping equalize opportunity in the way American schools are supposed to do is not just a frustration. It haunts us. Sometimes teachers are mystified, demoralized, or even totally overwhelmed by the stubborn persistence of the gap, just as Mr. Wilton is.

The achievement gap is usually defined by lower test scores for African American and Latino students as compared to white and Asian students. The exhortation "Close the Achievement Gap!" is the current dominant catchphrase in urban school reform: it is constantly invoked, sometimes honestly and sometimes, I believe, hypocritically, in our public discussions. The goal of "reducing the gap" is used to justify what I consider to be some profoundly counterproductive practices—practices that damage students and worsen the problem they set out to address.

The current response to the achievement gap, and to the No Child Left Behind (NCLB) policy, requires educators to analyze reams of data—standardized test after standardized test, with results "disaggregated" to display all subgroups (by race, socioeconomic class, gender, and language background). At BAA we are drowning in this sea of data. Dozens of three-ring binders give us page after page of numbers and charts, issued by every possible agency of the federal, state, and local governments, not to mention think tanks and universities. This level of analysis is supposedly necessary in order to improve funding levels in urban schools. It is accountability talk: dollars will come if school districts show where they are doing well or have weaknesses. However, I have not observed additional dollars pouring into school systems that are commensurate with the time and energy spent on sorting and sifting students' test scores into various racial subgroups. I wish the binders would arrive with huge checks tucked inside.

In most schools, urban or suburban, there are still unacceptable achievement gaps between poor and middle-class students; between white and Asian students; and between white and African American and Latino students. The number of African American young men who are in special education is still too high; Latino males do worse than most other subgroups, and the academic gaps between rich and poor continue to grow.

When I read the current national or state NCLB policies, I notice that despite the reams of research, there is almost no space or time to talk about who our students *are* in terms of their race, culture, gender, language, and social class. Certainly the kids are labeled and broken down by these categories, but questions about how racial and cultural differences actually impact learning—as opposed to test scores—are ignored.

When "scientifically valid" tests or curricula are touted as the silver bullet to success, time for such discussions is neither allowed nor valued. Teachers in my district are paid for *eighteen hours* of professional development time *per year*. Can you imagine any other profession that is deemed to be "in crisis" providing only eighteen hours of paid planning time to address the crisis? To me, this is ludicrous at best and insulting at worst. Where are the opportunities for teachers and administrators to study and absorb the research literature? Where is the opportunity for teachers to discuss their actual classroom experiences and then construct a plan of action for improved student achievement? When is there time to discuss the hugely complicated nature of our students' lives and the inequities of our society as a whole? Why, in many instances, is this kind of talk deemed to be taboo in our schools?

"But just talking isn't going to close the achievement gap I'm facing in my school!" says a colleague of mine whose school has not made AYP (adequate yearly progress) for three years. "How is *talking* going to raise the test scores in my school and get my school away from the threat of state takeover? We are instituting test prep for all students who are in the 'failing' or 'needs improvement' category on the state tests. We are going to focus on skill development each and every day!" I hear in her voice the determination to *do something*, which I admire and respect. I wonder, though, if she has thought carefully about the efficacy of her actions.

I sigh, listening to my colleague's plans. I have heard them many times in different forms. "More test prep" is the response that seems most expedient, but while student test scores may go up for the short term, since students recall skills are emphasized, "test prep" does not provide students with the kind of skills necessary to successfully learn more complex problem solving when memorization isn't an option. Clearly, "just talking" is not a sufficient strategy to close long-standing achievement gaps, but unless educators embark on the difficult conversations, we will continue to implement the newest district or even school-based "tactic of the month" without ever undertaking the kind of thoughtful actions needed to improve urban schools. I want my colleague to try a different strategy. What would happen, I want superintendents and principals to ask themselves, if we provided regular, sacrosanct opportunities for our teachers to discuss what is going on in their classrooms and their relationships with students and their families? How might that approach work? And what would it take to try?

SO WHAT HAVE WE ACTUALLY DONE AT BAA?

At BAA we provide opportunities for teachers to talk openly and frankly. As a principal, I guard this time against the demands of our schedules, which can easily encroach on them because, in the moment, we feel that getting through the days with kids is more important than talking to each other. We continue to structure time for teachers to examine their own practices and beliefs in order to discover if they are unwittingly contributing to the achievement gap. We believe that only this careful and thoughtful exploration of our students' achievements and our own teaching practices will allow us to imbue the widely heard refrain "hold our students to high standards" with any meaning. We are certain that only self-conscious, difficult discussions about race and class, and the eventual decisions that result from those discussions, will ultimately change our schools and our students' abilities to achieve.

Thus, Ms. Torres and I took Mr. Wilton's worries about his students and their skewed achievement results very seriously. In order to ensure that our data was not coming from just one teacher, Ms. Torres put together graphs of all our honor roll students over the past two terms. We noted disappointing similarities. For example, not one African American male was on the high honor roll (all As). When Ms. Torres and I sat down to look at the graphs, I expected to see what I saw, and yet those columns, so skewed by race and gender, felt like a personal failure. When I opened BAA, I had had such confidence that we would see different trends. I believed that all our hard work would result in definitive proof that arts could truly be the way to close the achievement gap. I felt sure that we had the right hook and we could build from there. I still think we can, but we are certainly not there yet. What I fear is returning to the status quo. That is what I hear when my colleague says she will institute test prep for all. That is the easy answer. Yes, test scores might go up for a testing cycle, but will students really learn the logic behind solving those problems whose answers they memorize? Moreover, I'm not convinced that with a heavy diet of test prep our students will learn the skills necessary to succeed in college.

Therefore, when Ms. Torres brought the honor roll data to the leadership team, we already had some history of talking about assessment and data with one another. "I have separated the honor roll information by race, gender, and socioeconomic background, as well as arts major," she told the team. "You can see the gaps. Our white and more middle-class students are outperforming our students of color in large numbers. The obvious question here is, What can we do? And, in particular, what can we do to improve the achievement of our young men of color?"

FIRST, WE TALKED AS ADULTS ABOUT THE PROBLEM: THE LEADERSHIP COMMITTEE DISCUSSIONS

We had no expectations that the process would be easy, but we were not at all prepared for how contentious and all consuming it would turn out to be. In the following pages, I present a sampling from our conversations to show that despite the dramatically disparate views and some awkward moments, the outcome was ultimately instructive and generative.

In an early discussion, Mr. Rojas, a humanities teacher of Dominican descent, began by saying that he felt it was important to understand achievement data in terms of what he called "dominant ideologies"—patriarchy, heterosexism, capitalism, and racism. "Without a larger understanding of these societal forces, we will provide only piecemeal solutions."

Mr. Babson, one of our newer math teachers, countered that he did not feel competent initiating a conversation about dominant ideologies since his training was in mathematics, not sociology. "Math isn't about culture and values," he said flatly, "it's about numbers and the power that one acquires from using those numbers. Look, I quite understand that I have a privileged position in this society as a white male—one of the reasons I became a math teacher is because I believe that numbers are color-blind."

Mr. Wilton spoke. "My job as a teacher, and as an African American man who lives in the, quote, minority community, end quote, is to continually connect my work in the sciences to race and racism, culture, class, language, you name it. My whole life I've known that student achievement is related to systematic oppression or what you call dominant ideologies," he said, nodding toward Mr. Rojas.

Mr. Wilton continued, his eyebrows arched, challenging the group to counter him. "So I consciously use my classroom and my teaching as a way to counter the stereotypes that are rampant among my students and the larger society. For example, I encourage my students to voice questions such as 'how come women...' and I let them fill in the blanks. Or 'how come...' and I encourage them to say blacks, gays, Asians, Latinos, et cetera. I want them to use class time to think about how race and culture and language play out in everything we do, and still learn the material I'm teaching.

"I think I've been reasonably successful with opening up those conversations for my students, but it's still not enough. When I look at who is doing well in my class and who is not, I know that we what we're doing just isn't making enough of a difference."

Mr. Hoyos stated passionately that there was no way he could fixate on whatever dominant ideologies currently existed. "I came to this country as a poor immigrant from Peru, and if I had let politics or economics oppress me or determine how far I could advance then I wouldn't even be here today. The only thing that really matters is understanding our students' lives and their culture and then coming up with teaching strategies that help them have better and better skills. Focusing on the societal stuff that we can't change won't get us anywhere." He looked directly at Mr. Rojas and Mr. Wilton. "In fact," Mr. Hoyos continued sternly, "I think these kinds of dominant ideology conversations get us nowhere and will just tear us apart. We need to focus on what's in front of us—how to be better teachers and go from there."

"Are we getting somewhere with our discussions?" I asked Ms. Torres later. "I worry about all the opposing viewpoints in our faculty. How can we bring everyone together?"

"I have faith that we are asking the right questions. We know this is hard work. If it were easy, we wouldn't be in it!" Ms. Torres reminded me. "You should have seen my dining room table covered with all that data. I was so discouraged. But then I look at Frankie and Luis and I remember what they were like four years ago. They will both be attending community college in September. We didn't think they'd even finish high school before. And Nilda—remember how we'd almost given up on her? She's applying to law school now. We have to keep remembering how far we've come."

"I know you're right. You always know how to put a student face on the numbers. But I worry a lot about the dissension that I feel these data conversations bring. And I know we are in this for the long haul. There are no easy answers."

"Listen," Ms. Torres began, "the numbers tap into our feelings, our own upbringings, and experiences. That's why we've committed to talk about issues of race and gender and language and culture. It's all connected."

We reassured each other that come what might, we had to trust that the discussion would ultimately help us go where we needed to go.

As the months went by, faculty on the leadership team continued to raise questions and concerns. At another meeting, Mr. Rodriguez, a teacher who had been one of the few Puerto Rican students to graduate from his Boston public school and then attend college, worried that because we had such differences in our own experiences and backgrounds we would never be able to come up with a unified approach to counter the achievement gaps that were in front of us. "The problem here is that we don't all hold the same values," he insisted. "We can't make excuses for our students. We have to agree that we won't allow anything—not race, language, poverty, none of it—to get in the way of our students achieving. We can't make excuses for them. We have to tell them that they can and will make it.

"We can only do this if we agree on certain values together. And I'm including things like no cell phones, hats, Walkmans, gum.... It's all part of the same equation. If kids look like bums and are allowed to break the rules—no matter how stupid we might think the rules are—then how will they see the point in working hard? I absolutely believe there's a connection between sticking to our community standards—our rules—and doing well in school. We all agree that these data are unacceptable. So we must move from these discussions to actual classroom and corridor and community practices that *will* narrow the achievement gap!"

"I'm not making excuses," Ms. Bonilla, our outreach coordinator and another Puerto Rican educator who was the first in her family to graduate from high school, began. "But you have to remember that our students have never been in a school environment like this one before. They come from very traditional schools. There's never been a school where reading, writing, and math can be taught, in part, through the arts, and where the students are expected to do so many different things. Our students are used to worksheets and workbooks. Remember that—"

"But what about Delvin and Andre and Kenny? Won't they lose out while we are building the school?" Mr. Wilton cautioned. "I just feel that even though they are passionate about the arts, they can't read. And I don't know *how* to teach reading. I'm a science teacher."

"Could I finish, please?" said Ms. Bonilla. "We also have to keep paying attention to their neighborhoods, and their families. Most of their parents haven't even finished high school, and they've certainly never been in one like this! My own mother wouldn't have known how to respond to BAA if any of her kids were here. She expected school to be about reading, writing, and doing sums. Don't get me wrong, I'm fully aware that too many students aren't learning and are dropping out of the old system. I absolutely think our approaches are the right ones."

"But I don't want us to just do a lot of talking," Ms. Roman, an arts teacher, insisted at the beginning of another discussion. "And I don't think we can take action until we understand how we might be a part of all of this. As African American educators, that's what we've learned the hard way throughout history. I know we're all good people here, but we really need to understand who our kids are—I mean culturally, racially, what and where they come from. That's what Ms. Bonilla was saying, too. Do we know their neighborhoods? Where they hang out after school? Sometimes I feel like we are just too academic or intellectual. And I don't mean to put anyone out there. But we have to get 'down' and really understand how to change ourselves before we can help change our students."

"I'm not here to share my personal feelings about race or culture with all of you," Ms. Melendez countered, clearly trying to stay calm. "I think the focus has to be on the students. Not 'getting down,' as you say, with each other. We have to work with each individual student. That's what we are here for—the students. But me talking about I how feel about race or class or whatever isn't going to help students feel good about themselves as scholars. We want to give students power and excitement and pleasure with intellectual successes as well as creative endeavors. I leave my personal stuff at home. I'm a professional here."

"I actually agree with both of you," Mr. Creighton broke in. "I think we're too soft on our kids. We let them use their race or their lack of money as an excuse. I came up hard just like our students, and this school offers so much more than what I had growing up. I was lucky to just have shoes to go to school. That was down South. My parents worked as sharecroppers. I tell my students, 'I can't go home with you and do your homework for you. I already earned my degree. Now I'm here to help you earn yours, but laziness and procrastination won't cut it in my class.' That's what I say. I think too many of us coddle our kids. It's a mean world out there and we have to get them ready to face it. Success for my students is determined by how much work they put into mastering the content, not by how they deal with their racial or ethnic or linguistic background," he finished emphatically.

Ms. Sampson had hardly spoken up during our many months of discussion. At last she shared her perspective. "You know, I think it's a whole lot more complicated. I'm not saying we let poverty be an excuse, but I sure think we have to understand its pernicious effects on our students. Yes, we offer a lot of opportunities, certainly more than most urban schools, but there is always more we can do. I'm just saying that the system is rigged in favor of the middle class and it's our job to rig it the other way. My high school had a college fair, too—just like we do, but my parents took me to visit colleges as well. And yeah, we're black! My mom asked me about colleges. My mom's friends asked me. There were discussions in my house about the advantages of historic black colleges versus other ones. There was discussion about how to apply for financial aid.

"There was a whole circle of people in my life making sure that I was thinking about college and that I would go. In my family there was never a moment when I would have even had a chance to think about not going to college. It was just expected of me. How many of our kids grow up with that kind of circle of expectations and experiences? We make it sound like our kids are especially ungrateful or unmotivated or hate doing homework more than other kids, but hey, *most* kids are that way. It's just that in middle-class circles there is a lot of protection against the damages of procrastination. If you are middle class, it doesn't matter if you screw up, because your family will bail you out. You know how they ask on college applications if you are a legacy? Our kids don't even know what that means!"

The conversation went back and forth for weeks and months between those teachers who felt that we had to "get down" and analyze our own "stuff," and those who felt that to do so was a waste of time and an intrusion on personal space. Other teachers felt that questions related to dominant ideologies were political or societal in nature and thus impossible to solve in a school setting. Still others felt unprepared or too insecure to venture out of their own comfort zone and into the land-mined terrain of race. And some teachers were insistent on taking action.

Toward the end of the year, Mr. Rojas spoke impatiently about how he wanted something to happen and to happen now. "We've been sitting around and talking about this stuff almost all year long. I just can't take this anymore—I want to *do* something. It's not about blaming our kids, like has been said, but we've got to find ways to get our young males of color to 'own' their educations. We have to take action and we have to do it now.

"I propose that we have an assembly for all the men of color and have an open discussion. All the male faculty of color will be there, too. We'll act as facilitators. We must listen to our students. We must start with what they are saying about these data. From there we'll figure out the action steps."

Mr. Wilton jumped up. "Yes! This is what I'm talking about. This is a great idea. Our kids need to talk about these issues with us and with each other."

There was silence among the other teachers. Everyone respected both men. Was Mr. Rojas's suggestion a possible solution to the impasse in our ongoing conversation?

Mr. Babson, the math teacher, asked uncomfortably, "What will I do with the students left in my classroom? It'll just be the black females and all the white students. I don't know how to deal with that."

He pressed on with his worries. "What about students who are biracial and don't know which group to identify themselves with? Where will they go?"

"I'm not sure the issue is as simple as just getting the men of color together," said Mr. Garcia, a humanities teacher. "For instance, I think many of our young men of color are also questioning their sexual orientation. We can't just isolate race. I'm not saying that this is a bad idea. We did this kind of thing when I was a student in a large comprehensive urban high school where there were a lot of students, like me, who were Mexican American or Chicano, but it's different here. When we do things as a faculty and a school, we really think about the repercussions, and we plan for that. We need to really *plan* for these meetings. There has to be a clear structure and a clear plan of action."

Mr. Hoyos was apprehensive about pathologizing the students of color. "Will this get taken the wrong way if we ask all the students of color to come together and discuss what's wrong with them? I'm just not sure this is the right approach."

This discussion, as had so many others, raised many more questions than it answered. Mr. Rojas was frustrated. So was Mr. Wilton. They were ready to run with their idea. They thought that simply bringing the male students of color together in an affinity grouping would be powerful in and of itself. A good listener, problem solver, and community builder, Mr. Rojas wanted *something* to happen. He wasn't prepared for the variety of opinions that surfaced, and he was taken aback by the disagreement even among the faculty of color.

o   o   o

I recount this story of our deliberations in such detail to show how difficult it is to talk about race with the goal of improving student achievement. Mr. Rojas's frustration is real, just as the hesitancies and fears that other teachers express are. I think school leaders shy away from asking faculty to undertake these difficult race conversations for fear of getting mired in personal issues and creating unhappy teachers who feel their ineffectiveness or their anger too acutely.

In fact, Ms. Torres and I felt that many approaches were necessary. The challenge was how to structure our faculty professional development time so that we could both make headway with students and the persistent "achievement gap" *and* begin to break down barriers and preconceptions among ourselves. We as adults would have to find ways to talk as a faculty about our own feelings as they related to race, gender, culture, class, and language. Once we had found those ways (and our first year's experience showed us how challenging that would persist in being), our talk had to be directly linked to classroom practices and student achievement. It would be a delicate balance to maintain, particularly for a school so early in its development. However, we were convinced that unless we achieved this balance, we would be unable to narrow the "achievement gap."

Ms. Torres returned to the data she had provided for the team over a year ago, and acknowledged the variety of opinions and the range of emotions that had surfaced among the faculty members. "Look, these are never easy conversations to have. Where else in our lives do we sit in mixed groups—mixed in every way: by race, gender, social class, language background, and culture—and try to solve a problem that few urban educators have been able to solve?

"However, I am convinced that by looking at our own data and then at the services and programs we provide, we'll come up with even better approaches for our students." Ms. Torres took a breath and started again, "We also need to look more closely at our own experiences and backgrounds and see how we can help one another build stronger relationships with our students. That's come up throughout our discussions. We're already beginning that work. It is not my sole responsibility to relate to and understand our Puerto Rican students just because I'm Puerto Rican, but if I have insights that might help a colleague who is not Puerto Rican, I have an obligation to share those. To blame, shame, or attack one another will never help us improve student learning. We must be committed together." I was applauding inside as Ms. Torres spoke. I could see other heads nodding around the table.

She continued, embracing everyone with her clarity. "We need to keep asking questions such as: What else might we bring into a student's life to improve the current situation? Is it slow and steady support (like a reading tutor)? Or is it triage such as a family conference? Is it more time in the Learning Center for Keisha? Should Kenny drop an academic course? Or are the solutions much more comprehensive? Must we all become more experienced reading teachers? And do we need to better understand why males of color are the largest group in our attrition data? Not only do they have the worst grades as a group, but we lose more of them than any of this subgroup of kids."

"I have a sense that the answer is yes to all of those questions," I said. And I am so lucky to be on this journey with a colleague and friend who is so smart and astute and willing to make mistakes, I thought (and think daily). I know that our work will be so much better because we are doing this together. I could never handle it all by myself, especially as a white woman.

As we discussed strategies, one of the representatives on the leadership team, Mr. Pai, suggested that we read a short article by Joshua Aronson called "The Threat of Stereotype," which was published in

Educational Leadership in November 2004. The article describes the negative effects of stereotype threats on achievement. Aronson and Claude Steele's research, done mostly with college students in testing situations, demonstrates how intellectual capacities and motivation can be compromised when social contexts threaten basic motives—such as sense of competence, trust in others, or feelings of belonging. We were living much of what the article described.

One paragraph particularly resonated for us:

> Studies also indicate the benefits of teaching students to conceptualize their intellectual abilities as expandable rather than fixed. Stereotypes impose on students the notion that their difficulties reflect an unalterable limitation, a bell curve view of abilities that says that some people are born smart and others dumb. When we teach students to reconsider the nature of intelligence, to think of their minds as muscles that get strengthened and expanded—*smarter*—with hard work, we find that their negative responses to stereotype threat diminish.

After a lengthy discussion ourselves, in which we were even willing to ask if or how *we* might be unintentionally reinforcing stereotypes, we agreed to begin observing one another in our classrooms, paying particular attention to interactions with our young men of color. Teachers generated specific questions for their colleagues' observation notes. Some teachers wanted to know if they meted out discipline equitably. Were they quicker to reprimand young men of color? Or, conversely, did they ignore their negative behaviors more often than other students? Other teachers wanted to know if there were defined patterns on how students participated in class. Did teachers call on one group of students more than another? Our intention was to shine a sharp light onto our own teaching and carefully notice, in lots of written detail, what effects our actions might create.

One teacher was surprised to find out from the observation notes that she called on the young men of color in her class more frequently than any other group because they were the loudest. She had never realized that until we started this process of careful observation. Another teacher was gratified to learn that her students participated in discussions equally. She had worried that her young women were dominating, but learned through the feedback that this wasn't true. Asking teachers to pay attention to one particular group of students helped us all think more deeply about our teaching and how our actions implicitly or explicitly affect student outcomes.

To get the students' perspectives, Mr. Pai and Mr. Rojas worked with some of them to make a documentary responding to some of the questions raised in the article. In the finished film, students interviewed classmates and asked them about their perceptions of how or if their racial or ethnic identity connected in any way to success in school.

Interestingly, very few students who spoke agreed with the premises of the article. "My race has nothing to do with how I do in school," said one African American young man. "It's about how hard I try." Another student, a young white man, was shocked at the idea that race or gender could play a role in testing. "Are you kidding?! I never do well on tests, and I'm not doing very well in school either!"

However, one African American girl hinted at the article's themes. "Well, I don't know what to say about all this. I know there is a big issue about blacks and standardized tests. I've always done very well on them. I've also been told since I was little that I did. Maybe there is something about what you get told since you were in kindergarten or something. Everyone always said I did well, but my brother didn't. What's weird is that we are twins and so the same almost everywhere else."

After viewing this student-made film and digesting the results of the classroom peer-observations, the entire faculty decided to implement a specific strategy, Literature Circles, in order to help us, as teachers, to listen more closely to what our students were saying.

THEN, WE TOOK SCHOOL-WIDE ACTION:
LITERATURE CIRCLES FOR LISTENING

We often use Literature Circles at BAA. They are small, temporary discussion groups that focus on the same story, poem, article, or book. While reading, each member of the group prepares to take specific responsibilities in the upcoming discussion, and everyone comes to the group with notes that will encourage a rich discussion as well as allowing them to perform their specific task.

Literature Circles can also be conducive to using a fishbowl technique: placing some students in the center of the room discussing the assigned reading—the fish—and others on the outside listening and taking notes—the bowl. When Mr. Rojas proposed we prioritize race and gender by purposely placing our young men of color on the inside of the circle and all the other students on the outside, Ms. Baez said, "Wait a minute, I'm not sure that would work." Other teachers agreed. "I'm as uncomfortable with this idea as I was with having the segregated assembly." Mr. Rojas responded, "Look, we all agree that there is an achievement gap in our school. Just like in lots of schools. What I'm saying we need to do is purposefully address the issue. We have to talk about race. I want to try this strategy because I believe it will empower our young men of color to be in leadership positions in a classroom setting." Some teachers were still uncomfortable.

I worried we were at a stalemate again. Mr. Rojas asked me if he could address some of these worries by trying out his ideas using ourselves as guinea pigs. Working with the entire faculty, he put the male teachers of color in the middle of the room and the rest of the faculty and staff on the outside. The outside circle first listened to the inside circle, and then commented on what they had heard. We used the same reading that our students would be using—a controversial piece from the newspaper that argued about the causes and effects of school violence and race, while raising questions about whether the home or the school was responsible for teaching appropriate behavior to young people. It was powerful, just seeing all our male teachers of color involved in a discussion together. Their discussion was rich and fast-paced. I noticed that others, who had previously expressed discomfort, seemed more relaxed than I expected. "Maybe I could try this," Ms. Baez said. "I have to admit I've never thought about what it would be like to do this with students."

Over a period of two weeks, every writing seminar class used Literature Circles. I sat in on one classroom where the boys of color were in the fishbowl debating various themes from the article. "I think it's all from the media," Anthony said. "That's why we feel we're not supposed to be smart. The media always blames our upbringing, our homes, and our communities. That's what the author of this article is saying. Too many black people in jail, on the streets, jacked up on drugs. We think that's the way to make it. It's easy money."

Adam responded, "I know that's out there, but I wasn't raised that way. I don't agree with the author. I think this is always what people write about black people—how we're more interested in quick money instead of doing well in school. But I'm proud to be black and smart. I'm always on high honors. I couldn't go home if I didn't get straight As. That's just what my mom expects."

"Yeah, but how many of us are on high honors? Every time we do one of those assemblies, I can count. It's you and maybe one other. I'm just trying to make the connections," Sheldon said, shrugging his shoulders in an offhand way.

"Maybe that's because too many of you all are lazy. Maybe it has nothing to do with violence in the community or anything like this author is saying," Adam countered.

The boys in the circle broke out laughing, as did the African American girls outside of the fishbowl. Others shifted uncomfortably. But only the boys in the middle could talk now.

"I don't see how being smart has anything to do with race," Adam said.

"But you can't deny the pressures," Anthony broke in. "Come on now. Black-on-black crime. Easy money. Lousy neighborhoods. Lousy schools. I'm not talking about this school here. But most of my friends, in their schools, they don't even have doors on their bathrooms. Or toilet paper. And half their teachers are asleep. How can you learn in an environment like that? The schools are more to blame than parents and home life. That's what this article's talking about."

David, who had been sitting quietly all this time, shifted noisily in his seat. He didn't usually speak in class, but many students looked up to him. Like Adam, he had been one of the African American males on high honors before. "The way I see it is that this article reminds us that we can't understand why we are struggling as black males if we don't understand our past, our culture, our people. Not as an excuse. No, too many brothers do that, but we need to find perspective. That's why we are doing this discussion with just us in the circle. Too many times we have white people telling us how to act or why we have problems in our community. We need to do that for ourselves. And we need to do it now. I bet you that the author of this piece is white, too."

One of the white girls, Carol, on the outside of the circle, had her head in her hands. She sat still and rigidly. Her body language said, "I hate this conversation."

When Ms. Baez opened up the conversation to the outer circle, Carol was the first to speak. "I really think these kinds of conversations are stupid. What are we supposed to learn from this? We don't have prejudice here, and Anthony, David, Adam, and Sheldon are just like the rest of us. I don't get the point of having them in the inside and us outside. It just seems like it's about blaming white people again. I hate that. I hate that everything in this school is about race. It's not my fault that I'm white. I didn't do anything to anyone. And my family has really struggled. My dad doesn't even have work now."

Adam said, "Yeah, but it isn't about you personally. What David's trying to say is that as black people we've got to know our own history. For him, that's the connection he made from the reading. And he was talking about why it was good to have the circle with just black males. Yes, slavery was back in the day. But it happened. And it was white people who did it. It's not about blaming you or your family. But it is about understanding. Sometimes that hurts."

As I left the classroom I thought about what a powerful interchange I had just witnessed. I wondered if we would find more ways to "segregate" our students in order to hear them better. I also wondered if there'd be any repercussions from parents. Would there be complaints?

Later, Ms. Baez reflected on the situation with colleagues in a staff meeting. Her reflections represented what many of us had noticed and felt in our own classrooms. "I was so pleased to see the boys of color so invested in the topic, but I was disturbed by some of the white students' responses, particularly Carol's. It was really hard for me to listen to her. This was a completely new experience for her, and it made her, and others, squirm. They are used to being the fish—the leaders—they are in the middle of the circle all the time. Just like many of us white teachers. But this time they were observers—on the outside. That's what was killing Carol. She is always the talker. Kids who don't always lead or don't have their opinions listened to that much were center stage. David rarely talks, even though kids respect him. Neither does Anthony talk. It was disconcerting for a lot of my white students to just listen and to listen to strong words. That doesn't mean it was a bad experience, but it was awkward and sometimes embarrassing for them and for me. So where are we going from here?"

Ms. Baez was nervous; her original concerns had been borne out. And, her question was a good one: what were the Literature Circles teaching us and how would that play out (if at all) in increasing the academic achievement of these young men?

Faculty talked about how we could expand the role of the "fish" another time to the girls of color, or only to the white students. We talked about the risks we had taken to create safe places for students to have these kinds of conversations. We talked about how we had feared that by singling out boys of color, we wouldn't be able to handle the range of student responses. Even though some teachers and students had felt uncomfortable, the experience had been generally positive. The Literature Circles were helping us work through our own discomfort about allowing race to be a focus of our own professional development.

We saw that Literature Circles created both a safety net and a very structured approach to both analyzing a text and entering into racially charged discussions. And we realized how much our students had to say about the links between race and achievement.

THEN, WE LISTENED CAREFULLY TO WHAT STUDENTS HAD TO SAY BEYOND THE LITERATURE CIRCLES: LEARNING FROM THE STUDENTS AS THEY WORKED IN THE ARTS

As we evaluated our work in Literature Circles and learned from our mistakes and successes, we quickly realized that our students were having similar conversations, whether faculty led them or not, about race, class, gender, and culture. In fact, of course, students had been having these conversations all along. Why were we, the adults, so nervous and afraid and even embarrassed, when students were quite open to talking about these "hotbed" issues?

In the semester after the Literature Circles, the number of young men of color on the honor roll went up. It would be absurd to suggest that somehow the school-wide Literature Circles caused the change. This would be insulting, in fact, to the young men themselves, who did so much work to improve their grades. I suspect, though, that opening up these conversations had a more subtle, but powerful effect that far outlasted the activity itself. I see that day as a moment when the school's attitude about race and achievement shifted in an incredibly important way, and I feel its reverberations in many of my interactions with BAA faculty and students.

During a visual arts exhibition, Sara showed me the small bust she'd done, "I Am a Black Woman." It was her "Witness and Legacy" monument. This is an assignment for all tenth-grade visual artists.

With her skin glowing and her braids tightly woven to her scalp, Sara explained, "There are too many African American women who feel shame at looking like me. It shouldn't matter what skin tone or what kind of hair you have. We don't need to divide up over these things. But that *is* what goes on in the black community. I'm trying to have this little sculpture speak to that." Looking at Sara's work and listening to her, I was reminded, again, about the importance of ensuring that adults and students in schools can think and talk about issues of race. Recently Sara returned for an alumni event and told me she has enrolled in hairdressing school. I asked her if she remembered her work from sophomore year that had made such an impact on me and others. "Of course I do!" she replied with a wide smile. "Maybe that's what cemented my interest in hair. Now, every day, I can make sure black women feel beautiful and proud."

Sara had had the time and space while in school to think about and find her own ways to address issues of importance to herself and her community. She had even found a way to turn her passions into employment. I felt proud.

A recent BAA drama production of *Fuente Ovejuna* opened the door for additional conversations about racism, violence, and injustice. The play, written by Lope de Vega, a contemporary of Shake-speare, takes place during the Spanish Inquisition (late 1400s) and is based on a true story. Fuente Ovejuna was a town ruled by a tyrant—Commander Gomez—who abused the peasants. The people, unable to defend their crops and homes from his greed, are finally shamed into action by one townswoman, but only after she is brutally raped. The peasants decide to kill the commander and then, when questioned, maintain silence—a collective "code of honor." Though they are horrifically tortured, each time they are asked, "Who killed the commander?" they say only, "Fuente Ovejuna did it"; that is, the town itself—the whole community—was culpable.

The BAA production was a testimony to the resiliency, empathy, and hopefulness of young people. The student actors brilliantly embodied the themes of honor, revenge, courage, and solidarity explored in this play. As the students left the stage after their curtain call, chanting, "Fuente Ovejuna did it!" their faces were lined with fatigue and pain. Behind the fatigue, though, I saw a great pride and a new kind of knowledge.

In the discussion that followed the performance, Patricia, a biracial senior who had acted in the play, said, "I know that this play mirrors life because oppression is happening everywhere in the world today. I do not agree with the townspeople cutting up the commander into little pieces, but there are other ways to have your voice heard today. Voting is one. And though a seventeen-year-old may feel helpless in this society, I just remember what a difference my art can make. I know that I am never helpless because I have the power to change people through the theater."

The performance also deeply affected the BAA faculty. One teacher wrote an e-mail to the cast: "Having grown up in the Basque country in the north of Spain, *Fuente Ovejuna* struck a chord in me. The depiction of torture numbed and haunted me for days. During the Franco era in Spain, my native language (Euskara, Basque) and thus my culture was forcefully suppressed....I left the play shaken and upset, knowing the torture did not end with the closing of the curtain...."

When I reported this story to the student actors, Duane responded, "Only a person like Lope de Vega, who went through this or witnessed such horror, can write this. This play reflects on our world today because tyranny, violence, rape, and torture still exist—it's just refined, especially in the United States. I turn on the news and I see and hear about my people shooting down each other. 'Be rude to an equal—that's stupidity. Be rude to a lesser man—that's tyranny.' That's what Captain Flores told the commander in our play, but the commander didn't pay any attention to him. But we have that going on right in my community every day. How do we talk about black-on-black crime?"

I mentioned to the group that only in the 1990s did Spain ever offer apologies for the many Jews and others who were tortured and forced into exile to escape persecution during the Inquisition. "Toledo is a town that was filled with Jews and Arabs in the 1400s," I told them, "and in a synagogue museum there is a small sign from King Juan Carlos of Spain, apologizing for the treatment of Jews in Spain during that era. Imagine: it took over five hundred years for Spain to officially issue an apology." Janayra, a junior, asked, "What do you think it will take for the U.S. to agree to reparations for African Americans?"

This began an intense and passionate discussion with many different opinions. The students were sometimes impatient with one another, but they were never dismissive. They listened to contrary opinions. They used their skills as members of an ensemble to understand what others wanted and needed to say. They waited while those who needed more time to formulate their thoughts spoke; they encouraged everyone to express their opinions, and, at times, they agreed to disagree. They used their wisdom and passions to talk across differences of race, class, culture, language, and gender. Art can make those connections. They used the techniques of talking from the text that they had practiced in Literature Circles and found that they applied equally well in theater class. At BAA we have wonderful role models in our artist-student body. They might just be the ones to help us all better understand how to talk about race.

SO DID THE BAA STRATEGIES WORK?

There isn't a one-to-one corollary. We have a sustained series of experiences that allows us to talk about race, and presto, the number of young men of color on the honor roll increases. Yet, as we have purposely and transparently focused on improving achievement for young men of color, more *are* edging their way onto the honor roll and gaining admission to more competitive colleges. It is still a bumpy road and, much as I'd like there to be one, I know there is no set formula. Maybe the young men of color, through these conversations, are encouraged to think more about why it is so difficult for them to succeed in school. I'd like to think that our many discussions subtly influence how other students in our school see and even encourage these young men. I'd also like to believe that our conversations and continual work even help teachers to see, without so much fear and shame, the ways in which they might still harbor stereotypes that hurt our students. But this effect will never be captured in pre- and post-intervention test results, the kind that superintendents and researchers love to see.

Our results are seen in the high graduation rate and college acceptances. But not all follow a conventional path. We recently honored seven BAA seniors at our August graduation. These were students who had not completed their requirements in time for the "regular" June commencement. While the August ceremony may not include all the pomp and circumstance of the June event, it is still as serious an occasion, complete with music and a graduation speaker. All the students participating in this particular ceremony had worked hard in their journey to arrive at this day. Most had attended summer school over the years, including this year. No matter how many times they had heard us say, "High school is not a timed test or a race to the finish line," they had all felt ashamed that they could not participate in the June ceremonies.

But here they were today with family members loaded with balloons, flowers, video cameras, and hugs. They were moving on. Ironically, each of these young men had been enormously successful in his art major. Yet they resisted the very idea of "school." They toiled to complete academic assignments on time. They had preferred to spend all day in the recording or dance studio to putting pen to paper. While their preference was shared by many of their fellow students, others were able to grit their teeth and turn away from things they wanted to do, at times, in order to complete academic work they needed to do. These students had ultimately made it to the "finish line," but not without exhausting struggles. Often, they had seemed to be fighting against their teachers, their school, and even themselves. I applauded our students' resilience. High school graduation is an important marker of success in our country. Yet, I knew that I was celebrating a mixed success.

These seven graduates were all African American men. I know that their academic skills are not as strong as they should be, even as I recognize their artistic talents and their engaging personalities. Renzo, one of the seven, is traveling soon to Africa to perform in three different countries. Even as I exulted in his opportunity, I asked myself: Does he have the skills to do a careful reading of his contract? Does he risk being taken advantage of by a manager? Surely, stories abound about fabulously successful artists who have not even graduated from high school and hit the charts. But many others never make it, hindered by their lack of skills beyond the arts. Would Renzo be one of the lucky ones, or would he become another statistic—

unemployed or underemployed, vulnerable to a life of criminality and substance abuse, a life that too often befalls black and brown urban men? I didn't want Renzo's life to teeter delicately on the sharp point of luck. I wanted his high school experience to have built a strong, solid foundation on which he could stand even if luck was not with him.

These seven students did not buy into BAA's vision of success by developing their skills in the manner that I thought they should or by graduating on time. They did not take advantage of the supports we provided as I had hoped they would. Even though I am happy to see them make it this far, disappointments lodge in my mind. I look inward and ask again: What are we not understanding about our students and ourselves? How can we do better? What can I do better?

Ms. Torres had earlier said to Mr. Wilton, "We are going to build success for our students from better understanding our frustrations." I continue to be quite certain that the best way to understand an issue is to ask about it. I suggested that a colleague interview these seven young men and ask them about their years at BAA. Some of our questions were: What helped you feel successful at BAA? What derailed you? How could we do better next time for you or another student like you? Do you think race or gender plays a role in your success in school? We videotaped the interviews so that we might use them in multiple ways to continue our professional development work.

Some of the most salient responses included one young man talking about the importance of trusting that his teachers would keep pushing him and not give up on him. This comment harkened back to themes in the Aronson article that we had read a few years before. Another participant simply said that only in his fourth year did he feel he belonged at our school. "I had seen my friend being asked to leave the school, but I didn't want to let you all down after you'd done so much. But mostly, I didn't want to let myself down or my mom." All of the interviewees talked about issues in their personal lives, such as lack of money in the family, a housing crisis, or the shooting of a loved one, that had kept them from graduating on time. We probed the students' thinking about race and gender, and each student talked in his own words about his understanding of being black, male, and a success in school. "I always wanted to finish stuff on time, but then I wouldn't and it would just get worse and worse. I had a hard time admitting I needed help." Another said, "I'm not sure that asking students to leave ever really helps anyone. It just proves what we can't do, not what we can do." It was that last statement that has kept us working harder and asking even more questions of one another. How can we continue to engage our students and even do things differently so that we don't lose them?

We need to look at the whole question of how our students and our faculty, and even our families, talk about school success. Does it mean something different to each of us? We have developed a new series of questions for one another about how each of us understands student success. Our goal is to learn from our students in order to improve our teaching.

WHAT'S NEXT?

I don't expect a miracle solution to appear overnight, but I do know I must learn from our past practices, as well as the successful work in other schools, in order to improve our future work. We need to continue to listen to our students and families. It certainly would be nice if all we had to do was use the next shiny, teacher-proof curriculum out of the box and watch the achievement gap disappear. Lots of schools and principals keep hoping that the next box or seminar or specialist brought in for in-service will have the key. But I firmly believe that critical evaluation and careful listening to students are a crucial part of how we will achieve more positive results for and with them. Slowly, we work to narrow the "achievement gap" we have in our own school. This is the hardest work in urban education. It is ongoing, relentless. It is not always linear. We are not always pleased with our results. And we are only too aware of the still unanswered and, in fact, *unasked* larger question: do we, as a society, have the appetite and the patience to take on the necessary work of reforming our schools?

At BAA we recognize that we cannot let our failures, or those of our students, deter us from the importance of continuing to speak up. We refuse to turn away from our discussions of race and class— no matter how difficult and complex. It would certainly be easier to ignore the many ways in which race, class, culture, and language connect to our students' achievements, but that would be to ignore our students themselves. I want to end this chapter with questions that all of us are asking, teachers, students, administrators, and parents, both urban and suburban, but not saying aloud.

1. Should we always have to talk about race? Is there a point at which it becomes too destructive and divisive? And what do you do when you see that coming?

2. How do you discuss race and class when you are in a school that consists of 99 percent of one race or socioeconomic background? Or what do you do in a school that has an overwhelming majority of kids of color and an overwhelming number of white teachers?

3. How do you, as a white principal, or a principal of color, model discussions about race so that everyone feels included and that their ideas matter?

4. What can educators do to lessen the motivation-sapping power of "stereotype threat"? How can teachers be more aware of it? What techniques—like cultivating the belief in kids that brain power is malleable, growable—are there for defusing it and counteracting it?

5. How can a high school fairly but seriously address the fact that kids from different racial groups may have had dramatically different preparation for high school work and high school test taking in grades one through eight?

The hard questions keep coming.

6.

An Open Door Is Not Enough

How can we learn to see the invisible barriers
students face and help students break them down?

Shanita was BAA's valedictorian and an extraordinary musician. In some ways she had put our music department on the map since she was the first one in our school to compete in district-wide, statewide, and then national music competitions. And each time she had done well. The faculty marveled at her skills as well as her poise and graciousness. Ms. Sampson, one of her music teachers, had called the school, literally sobbing with joy, when Shanita won first place in a national music festival. "She got the highest scores of anyone. And to think she was competing with students who have been doing this since they were old enough to walk, as well as studying with the most renowned teachers from across the country! It feels just like *The Little Engine That Could,* only I don't think Shanita ever doubted she could!"

While many young talented musicians come from families that have provided them with private lessons, private schools, costly and competitive ensemble experiences, and elite summer music camps since childhood, Shanita began her music studies for the first time in sixth grade in Boston Arts Academy's Saturday music program. Her older half-brother, Tony, had been a clarinetist at BAA, and Shanita attended his concerts and learned about our free program. She convinced her mom that if she attended the program she wouldn't watch so much television. So, at twelve years old, she started studying the clarinet because she said she wanted to be just like her older brother. Seven years later, as a BAA student and an accomplished eighteen-year-old musician, she was still inspired by the desire to play progressively more difficult pieces and to keep improving.

Shanita was first clarinetist in the school's small woodwind ensemble. She practiced conscientiously each day and never missed her private lessons with a graduate clarinet student from a nearby conservatory. She was a soulful player with an extraordinary understanding of melody and harmony and the very color of the sound. Her performance and interpretive abilities belied her youth.

Shanita's mother had never been able to come to hear her concerts, since now there were newborn twin sisters, as well as two other toddlers in the family. Shanita's mom's new husband, and the father of the new siblings, loved music, but he mostly was on the road and in between jobs, and couldn't ever show up for recitals. Shanita's half-brother, Tony, had left BAA a few years earlier and gotten a GED, his clarinet days seemingly forgotten. Shanita didn't talk about him much anymore, and when she did, it was with a tinge of resentment. He didn't show any interest in her music nor did he do much to support the family. Shanita's own father wasn't around either, but Tony's father, who had played the trumpet off and on, sometimes tried to come to her recitals. Shanita juggled a part-time job to help her mom, a rigorous practice schedule, and time for homework. She also found herself steadily more in demand as her success grew in the world of music, and any extra money she made from performances she turned over to her mother. For her college auditions she had perfected a Mozart concerto, and she had been accepted at a very prestigious conservatory on a full scholarship. She would be the first in her family to both finish high school and go on to college. All her teachers celebrated her accomplishments, and Shanita walked through the halls with a permanent smile, talking about how she would now study with one of the greatest clarinet teachers in the country.

But in the spring, Shanita received a letter saying that her conservatory scholarship had been rescinded because she hadn't sent in her deposit in time. Only as her teachers, Ms. Sampson and Ms. Richardson, unraveled the series of events did they realize that Shanita had been too ashamed to tell them that she didn't have the five hundred dollars necessary to make the deposit to hold her seat and the scholarship. Her teachers bemoaned the seeming impossibility of this event. Ms. Sampson, a veteran teacher, felt that she knew Shanita so well. Ms. Richardson, who had only joined the faculty a few years before, also felt that she had an open and trusting relationship with her. After all, they had taken her to competition after competition. They had stayed together in hotel rooms, stayed up late listening to bands at the international jazz festival, critiqued other high school groups together, and watched proudly as Shanita rehearsed with the Boston Arts Academy woodwind ensemble and served as assistant conductor for the big band. They had rejoiced together in her successes. They had spent hours helping her to prepare for her audition. She had the complete trust of her teachers and her peers.

Perhaps because of that very trust, Shanita had been reluctant to tell Ms. Sampson that she couldn't come up with the money. Ms. Sampson had done so much for her. How could Shanita let her down now and admit to not having enough for a deposit? Perhaps Shanita worried that Ms. Sampson would think that her time had been wasted. When Shanita eventually did tell Ms. Sampson about her dilemma of not having the money for the deposit, it was past the deadline and there was little that Ms. Sampson, or anyone else, could do. Ms. Sampson called the head of the conservatory and tried to explain Shanita's situation, but though the head was sympathetic, she explained that it was now too late. In fact, heartbreakingly, the head told Ms. Sampson they would have waived the deposit fee if they had only known in time, but the conservatory head and admissions director had assumed that Shanita didn't want to attend, and the scholarship had been reallocated to another deserving student. The entire music department faculty and I were outraged that our talented and hard-working student would be denied an education at the institution of her choice.

This situation taught us, sadly, that we didn't yet understand enough about our own assumptions about what students would need in order to be able to access social, political, and educational possibilities. When Ms. Sampson told me what was going on I was absolutely furious—first at the institution that wouldn't still accept her and then at myself for not checking in with Shanita and her teachers. Perhaps if I had gotten involved sooner I could have turned things around. I called the admissions head myself but got the same answer. I even called the president of another college whom I thought could exert pressure, but the decision had been made. I realized that in Shanita's case, we had inadvertently stumbled against our own middle-class experiences and ideas and had seen too late that no matter what we thought about our positive, close, and trusting relationship with this student, we had neglected to fully understand her circumstances.

Access is more than just providing opportunities: it is also about teaching students how to gain entrée into the system that controls those opportunities. To create access for our students we have to make visible the invisible threads of privilege that some students enjoy by virtue of social class, race, language, background, or gender. We can't leave the responsibility of deciphering the codes that prevent access in the hands of the students or their families. Shanita's barrier to access was not five hundred dollars. Ms. Sampson, or any of us, would have helped her overcome that barrier quite easily. The true barrier was an invisible one, created and maintained by two crucial forces: the student's shame and the teachers' and my own ignorance.

Teachers and guidance counselors would probably never think to ask if a middle-class family had sent in the deposit; they would assume that every family would do so. Middle-class children are, in fact, born into this kind of knowledge. Middle-class families know how the system works.

Ms. Sampson certainly understood that students like Shanita are not competing on a level playing field; otherwise, she would not have been so ecstatic at Shanita's success. Ms. Sampson knew how unusual it was to have a student with an extraordinarily developed musical ability who had not been raised with privilege. Even so, she had inadvertently overlooked how growing up without power or social knowledge might create invisible barriers to Shanita's future success.

Later, as she talked about this situation, Ms. Sampson, who had grown up in one of the few African American families in a solidly middle-class suburban community, remembered how her father had driven her at midnight to the post office so she would get her college application postmarked by the deadline. Ms. Sampson's father hadn't attended college, but her mother, a schoolteacher, had a college degree, and her maternal grandmother had been a schoolteacher down South. Ms. Sampson's family had some knowledge of the unspoken rules of access. As members of the middle class, they had internalized many of the mechanisms that allow privilege to perpetuate itself. There had been no neon sign at Ms. Sampson's high school announcing that only one post office in the city was open until midnight. But it had been a topic of conversation between other families on the sports fields, at family nights, and high school events, and during guidance meetings. These were just pieces of information that middle-class families knew and assimilated. Almost like a second skin.

In urban schools, teachers and counselors have a special obligation that goes beyond their job descriptions on paper. My life as an urban teacher and leader has led me to the passionate belief that urban teachers have a responsibility to remedy injustices perpetrated by race, class, gender, and language origin prejudices. This means learning a repertoire that is beyond teaching content and that includes the knowledge of culture, family backgrounds, and students' prior experiences.

For urban educators, stories such as Shanita's are all too common. Even when we know that social class (or privilege) is distributed unequally in our school systems in ways that are unfair to poor children or children of color, it is still too easy to be swept up into the belief that if we just work "harder" with our students and prepare them "better," entrance into elite institutions will be theirs for the taking. We forget about the pernicious effects that poverty and class prejudice can have on our students. Even when we do know, and do think about these issues all the time, our very knowledge can blind us. We think we know so much, but then those deeper layers, the invisible ones—come up and surprise us.

We forget that an open door is not enough. The formal opportunities may exist—the scholarships, even the acceptance to competitive colleges or universities (although there are still too few of these available to our students)—but the knowledge of how to truly avail oneself of those opportunities is often missing. We, as teachers, might work hard to open doors for our students, but for those students to learn how to open the doors themselves, and then walk through them, requires an understanding of conventions that are often unspoken. Our job, as educators, as believers in American ideals of equality, is to make all of those unspoken conventions visible and navigable. That is the only way to have a truly level playing field.

Middle-class and white teachers, myself included, and even middle-class teachers of color like Ms. Sampson, often forget that there are things that we will simply miss because of our own limited experiences or lack of awareness of the barriers that class or race can impose. It is certainly *not* a guarantee that educators of color will understand all the nuances or cruelties of poverty. Even though 50 percent of our BAA faculty members are teachers of color, and many are in the first generation in their families to attend college, they, too, can overlook a cultural, socioeconomic, or race-related roadblock that a student might experience. We try to create equal opportunity for all of our students, as we should. We don't always get it right. We will learn from our mistakes with Shanita. But we will also have to remember that learning from Shanita doesn't mean that we can rest easily. Other situations that we fail to completely comprehend will occur. When BAA staff talks about breaking down barriers, we now ask each other the question, "Have you sent in the deposit?" We use the question as a metaphor to represent all the invisible barriers we may have missed, so that we can push ourselves and each other to learn even more, to ask questions that might embarrass our kids, to use our failure with Shanita to inspire successes in the future.

Shanita's story has a bittersweet outcome. She is attending a state college, pursuing a degree in psychology. She does not have the opportunity to study music at her school, but she says she still tries to play. Without a good music teacher, she may not be able to live out her true passions or potential. In BAA terms, we failed Shanita.

Preparing students to be successful in the college admissions process means working with them in ways that we, as teachers, may never have thought about. This is not the work that teachers are prepared for as they study for their education degrees. How many math or music teachers expect to be teaching their students how to fill out financial aid forms, or to be driving them around to visit colleges? I know that many teachers might initially respond to the call to learn more about students' lives and to involve themselves with students' preparation for the future at this level with real resistance: "That's not my job," they might say, or "I'm not the guidance counselor or the social worker." Nevertheless, I think principals need to engage *everyone* on staff to believe that all of us have a responsibility to help with college and life after high school. What kind of structures and professional development do principals need to create in order for teachers to change their expectations without being utterly overwhelmed? How can we help make room for this work in teachers' lives, rather than going the unfair route of simply asking them to add another huge burden of time and effort to their jobs? How can we train teachers for this work, just as they are trained to plan lessons and manage their classrooms? And, perhaps most crucially, how can a principal convince teachers that their jobs will be more satisfying if we are all working at this together?

Ricardo, a BAA senior, couldn't figure out his financial aid for college. His advisor knew that Ricardo's mother was in jail, but assumed that his grandmother was his legal guardian. We learned late in the application process that his mother was still his legal guardian and would have to sign all of his financial aid forms. Ricardo had to arrange to see her in jail, which was a two-hour ride away and not accessible by public transportation. No one in his family had a car. Although Ricardo communicated well with his teachers, and especially with his advisor, Beth, who had practically sat on Ricardo to get him to write his college essay, the complexities of his family situation caused him to miss deadlines for his first choice of college, and he ended up at a college that was not one of his top four choices. We might have learned the importance of asking, literally, of all our students, "Is your deposit in?" but we had not yet had a lesson on "what to do if your guardian is jail."

And yet these representative questions are exactly the ones we must ask and answer, or risk the fact that students like Shanita or Ricardo will not have access to the opportunities that they deserve. It is about systematically teaching our students how to get into "the system" and "work" it. I see now how the risk of embarrassment or shame works against both staff members and students themselves. It is so tough to ask questions that might get to the vulnerable, shame-filled heart of students' lives. We don't want to ever assume that our students are ashamed. Why should they be? They are strong, energetic, vibrant young people. But shame is lurking just below the surface and only by addressing it honestly will we get through the barriers.

What makes the process even harder for teachers, students, and parents today—and makes our efforts at pushing through them—is the fact that these barriers grow thicker and more unassailable each day. Tuitions continue to rise and the gate to higher education becomes narrower. The percentage of students who qualify for Pell Grants (federal grants for students from families with incomes of less than $40,000) continues to rise while enrollment of these students on many college campuses continues to fall. Universities and colleges raise their minimal SAT requirements in the race to be more selective and my students have one less opportunity available to them. We often hear from college admissions offices that if our students don't get the requisite SAT scores, they won't be able to compete academically. I wonder. I wonder if there is a will on the other side—the higher education side—to really embrace my students and provide the opportunities for access to and on these campuses.

I rage at how dismissive policy makers are of the need for increased funding for urban schools. Too many people in our country actually say and believe that money isn't the answer. It may not be *the* answer, but it surely helps if we can decrease class size, guidance counselor-student ratios, and increase library, physical education, and arts facilities. When families from higher incomes stop sending their children to elite private schools for the smaller classes and myriad offerings, perhaps I will believe that money doesn't matter.

AT BAA, HOW DO WE HELP KIDS SEE AND
OVERCOME THE INVISIBLE BARRIERS?

As a school, we try to offer a counterbalance to a class-based society. We know that our society is invisibly weighted toward the middle and upper classes. Norms and expectations are built around middle- and upper-middle-class values, and the middle class controls a significant chunk of cultural and social capital. If we expect our students to ever access the advantages of a middle-class life, then we must teach them how to do so. Everything from obtaining good dental care to good credit to learning interview skills to test-taking skills must be part of the curriculum.

There is no certainty of future success for students just by making opportunities available without providing the accompanying instruction that will allow students to truly take advantage of those opportunities. It is not enough to say, "There are many scholarships available for poor kids, but they just don't apply." I have learned from years of working with them that poor kids, like all kids, need the hand-holding, pushing, and relentless reminders from parents or teachers to "get those scholarship applications finished!" That is what many middle-class parents and schools provide for their students—the force-feeding, cajoling, and the insistence that this education can and will be yours.

Remembering my own experiences with applying to college has helped me confront my own ignorance. First of all, growing up in a family with two professional parents (one a teacher, the other a doctor), there was never a question that I would go to college—just which one. There was also never any doubt that I would go to a "good college." While my parents didn't drive me to visit colleges (I had to figure that out on my own) nor did they help me write my college essay ("We've been to college; this is your essay not ours!") I knew that any question I had would be answered. The dinner table conversation my junior and senior years was about the advantages and disadvantages of a whole range of "good colleges."

At BAA, under the leadership of our college and career counselor, Ms. Hairston, we have worked together as a faculty and staff to develop practices that encourage all our students to think about success after high school. I want to be sure we create in school something of what I, and so many like me, experienced at home.

Our expectation is clear: *all* BAA students will apply to college or enter a career-training program, which could include the military. Each year, Ms. Hairston organizes an assembly for ninth-, tenth-, and eleventh-graders to hear from alumni who now attend college and from graduating seniors about the college admissions process. It is one thing to have these discussions between teachers and students, but quite another thing when a graduate says, "Listen to Ms. Hairston when she says to apply for as many scholarships as you can. She knows where the money is!" or "Don't wait till the last minute like I did. Now I can't go to college full-time because I waited too long to apply for financial aid." Or "Don't be freaked out when all your roommates are white. It doesn't mean they are bad people. Remember you had white friends here!" The wisdom and advice from those "on the outside" is priceless for our students, and we tap it to provide a framework for them to think about colleges and careers after high school.

Ms. Hairston organizes an annual college fair at our school as well as an annual College Visit Day when all ninth-, tenth-, and eleventh-graders visit a college campus. It is a huge undertaking to arrange for three hundred and twenty students to visit area colleges, but we consider it part of our contract with students (and parents) to educate them early on about access to college. Most middle-class students have parents who take them to visit colleges, and even help them research different ones, which gives those students a special advantage. However, many BAA students don't have parents/caregivers who are able to participate in this way. So once a year, the entire faculty takes students to visit colleges both locally and out of state.

As I write this, I hear the objections from readers who teach in other urban public schools: "Yeah, fantastic, but where on earth are we going to get the resources to do this?" I have written grants to get money to support out-of-state trips, but we are fortunate that we live in a city with public transportation. There are many colleges just a short bus ride away. Duplicating this kind of experience at other schools would be challenging, but I don't believe that it is impossible for any school, and in our case the hard work we have done to create these opportunities and expectations has been worth it. The dividends—seeing our alumni experiencing success beyond high school—are priceless.

In advisory, students prepare questions to ask on the tours. After the visit, they debrief the experience. These visits, and the discussions surrounding them, are important in helping our students realize that they can be college material. Students also discuss the college admission process in advisory groups. Since they are mixed in advisory by grade level, this is another valuable way to share experiences and help younger students learn from older students.

We make it a requirement as part of both our eleventh- and twelfth-grade writing seminar classes that students sign up to take PSATs and SATs, and that they write many drafts of a college essay. In this way, the college application requirements become part of the school's academic obligations. We tell them that going to, for example, Bunker Hill Community College or Boston University are both valuable and viable options, but that students must understand early on the more demanding requirements for admission to an institution like Boston University. I know of a school nearby with many more students than my school that incorporates college essay writing into Senior English. What, I wonder, are the ways in a large school that the college application process can become part of the curriculum? And how, if a school doesn't have an advisory system in place, can more faculty share in the responsibility of helping students with life after high school?

I have found that the practices described above are crucial in creating a culture that says to all students, "You can graduate from high school, and you will. You can go to college, and you will." As advisors, we have found tactful ways of finding out about issues that might have an impact on the college admissions process, such as which students have parents who are not legally in the country. If a student never brings a parent/caregiver to a financial aid workshop, this may indicate that we need more information about that family's financial circumstances. And we continually keep in mind the lessons we have learned from Shanita and Ricardo.

HOW CAN WE MAKE ACADEMIC SUCCESS COOL?
DOES FEELING LIKE YOU BELONG IN THE
"SUCCESSFUL" GROUP REALLY MATTER?

At BAA, we keep asking one another these questions in faculty meetings. In my individual meetings with teachers we often end up brainstorming all sorts of answers to these questions. How do you teach access? Is it teachable? We've answered yes, and one of the ways we have been successful at teaching some of the skills of access at BAA is to introduce the idea of the importance of belonging to our school community. We believe that if our students learn to feel a sense of ownership and pride in their school, they will also feel more secure about venturing into unknown territories.

When our students see themselves as powerful learners with the ability to effect change in their own lives, academic success becomes cool. Our intention is to build a culture of shared success for all our students; therefore we celebrate them in very public ways. One staff member takes responsibility each year for covering a hallway-long bulletin board with portraits of the most recent graduates and descriptions of the colleges they now attend. Regularly, Ms. Torres and I use daily announcements to celebrate college admissions and scholarships. We want the entire school to know who got the Boston University four-year scholarship, who received the esteemed Presidential Scholarship from Berklee, and so on. Every quarter Ms. Torres and I take the high honors students to lunch. Beyond pure celebration, I talk to these students about why they think they have been successful and what they think would encourage more students to achieve high honors. We have learned that while our honor roll assemblies are good, we need to divide up students in several different ways. Previously we held "lower house" assemblies (grades nine and ten) and "upper house" assemblies (grades eleven and twelve). Students suggested different arrangements, such as grades nine and twelve together, or assemblies by arts major. In this way, they said, students would have different kinds of role modeling. They also suggested that we institute awards that were not purely academic or grade-based.

In chapter two, I described the Caught in the Act of Shared Values award that has become an important part of our fabric. After listening to our students' suggestions, we developed an award that is given once a year and called the Spirit of BAA. The teachers nominate and vote on students for the award, which acknowledges students who have shown extraordinary compassion, empathy, and citizenship to their fellow students. It is now as coveted an award as being on the honor roll. The recipients, who are few each year, are celebrated and photographed during honors assemblies and included in invitations to the high honors lunch. Students always put this award on their resumes and everyone at BAA talks about who the past awardees have been. The Spirit of BAA has developed some of the same panache as high honors. We have been proud, as a faculty, to note that often the students who receive the Spirit of BAA achieve membership in the honor roll in subsequent terms. There is something contagious about success. We have come to see that a student who is successful in one arena may allow that success to expand into another area.

Students like being cheered and they like the sense of acknowledgment that those cheers bring. Honor roll is a special club to belong to. In our school, it is, in fact, the "cool" club. Teachers at BAA have commented that sometimes African American males, in particular, feel that doing well in school is "acting white," though thankfully that has not been a dominant theme or refrain at BAA. At almost all of these assemblies we make it clear that for the following term we want to see more young men of color on the honor roll. We also make sure to acknowledge those young men who have made significant academic and artistic strides and earned honors grades. We are careful not to diminish our female students' successes, but we know that in order to change our overall student achievement patterns we have to state the problem aloud. We can't pretend that there isn't a disparity.

Often, after we dismiss the honorees and their families for the honor roll reception, either Ms. Torres or I keep the other students behind for a few minutes to remind them that we are proud of the way that they have warmly honored their peers. At a recent assembly I said, "I know it can be hard to sit here and see others get the applause, but I admire your ability to cheer your friends. I also know that to get honors grades here at BAA requires a lot of work. But I know more of you can achieve honors, especially those of you who are African American young men, and I know you want to. It matters that you get good grades because it will open up opportunities for you when you apply to college." I worry about speaking this way to a group of students. Will there be repercussions? Will some of my young students twist what I'm saying and hear these words as a putdown? I think about the Aronson article on stereotype threats again.

Worse will there be resentment on the part of some of my female students that we are focused more on young men than young women? I imagine all the ways that my students might misinterpret the messages I'm trying to send. I imagine that I might be sowing negative seeds of racial comparison. Still, I feel that it is important to hear the head of the school speak so specifically about student achievement in both racial and gender terms. I continue to hope—and believe—that my words sink in.

HOW CAN PARENTS HELP THEIR KIDS OVERCOME THE INVISIBLE BARRIERS, WHEN THE PARENTS THEMSELVES HAVE NEVER NAVIGATED THE SYSTEM?

Sometimes it's not enough that a student is smart; there must be more than raw intelligence to ensure student achievement. Family or extended family support is also crucial, and making achievement very public can help cement the connections between home and school.

Our parent coordinator sends special invitations to the parents/caregivers of those students who have achieved an honorable mention (As and Bs and only one C), honor roll (As and Bs), or high honors (all As). When time permits, she even makes special calls to a parent whose child is on honor roll for the first time. Sometimes she will ask Ms. Torres or me to make these calls because she knows a call from us might carry more weight as we ask parents to rearrange their schedules in order to attend the ceremony. We know that most of our students' parents work, so we try to give them enough notice, and we schedule the honor roll assemblies during the lunch hour. If a parent can't come, we ask for a grandparent, an older relative, or someone from another family who could celebrate the student's accomplishments. We have a number of parents who regularly come and celebrate three or four students at a time. We have experimented with doing one honor roll assembly a year in the evening as well.

At one of the small receptions we hold after the honor roll assemblies, I sat with a student, Daryl, and his mom. She was very emotional and proud of his success. "I didn't think I'd see this day again. All through elementary school he did so well and then middle school started...I don't know. He never made it to honor roll. This is just so wonderful. I know my son is smart and now you all do, too." Daryl beamed.

"I took away the video games," she told me. "I told Daryl, 'You show me you can get the grades and then we'll talk.' I know all these teachers here work too hard for him to be getting Ds and Cs. He begged me to come to the last show he was in. But I wouldn't. I told him I was coming up here when he got honors grades. I'm so proud of him today." So were we. We all felt joined in the common effort of building toward Daryl's success in high school and beyond.

I moved around from table to table during the reception, chatting with students and their parents, telling them how proud I was of their accomplishments. I sat with a group of young African American men and asked if they thought they could bring another friend over to the honor roll side. "Yeah, maybe," Nate said. "My friend Freddie was really close."

I wanted to know what had prevented Freddie from achieving honor roll status. Nate was thoughtful. "I'm not sure he studies as much as I do." Nate and I talked about whether there was any way that Nate could have an impact on that. "He and I could study together, I guess. I stay in the library most afternoons. And we live near each other. I could go over to his house. Next term we'll both be up there on the stage," he promised. "We'll both have our pictures for Term 3 on the wall." In fact, the following term, Freddie was on honor roll and BAA celebrated him. We also celebrated Nate for supporting him so well, and we celebrated Nate's mother and father who came for both boys. Freddie's mother hadn't been able to come, but we cheered for all the family members who were at the assembly. We made sure that everyone in the audience knew that this was Freddie's first time, but that it wouldn't be his last time. And we made sure that everyone at the assembly knew about the kind of support Freddie had received from his friend and his friend's parents. Freddie stayed on the honor roll almost every other term.

Urban schools often have to create from scratch the connections and networking opportunities that students in middle-class families take for granted. This means that at times it can seem as though we are running two schools—one for students and another for their parents/caregivers. In fact, we are. We try, as best we can, to give both groups the same message at the same time.

We hold meetings and workshops throughout the year, in the evenings and on Saturdays, with parents/caregivers and students, to ensure that everyone hears the same message about college entrance requirements and financial aid deadlines. We don't assume that either parents/caregivers or students understand the requirements for admission to a competitive four-year college. We see it as our job to teach our families about those requirements, and we try to demystify the whole college admissions process as much as possible. These are often first-ever discussions for parents and students. Parents frequently feel that since they have no firsthand knowledge about college admissions or even high school requirements, they can play no role in their children's education. However, because we insist that students bring a family member to these meetings, we begin to develop a shared vocabulary and understanding about the educational process. We want parents/caregivers to realize that we will be there to support them along the way.

Often, by the time students are in high school, they want to distance themselves from their parents, but our experiences have shown us that students will do better if parents are more involved. What might have happened differently for Shanita if her mom had been involved in the process? At a recent parent meeting, I was pleased when parents from a range of socioeconomic and linguistic backgrounds asked me about how we provide SAT prep and to explain "open honors" more thoroughly. If parents/caregivers don't understand what "open honors" means, their child might not take the risk of trying it. If parents/caregivers don't join their child and her teacher and advisor for conferences about student progress in school, we can't develop a partnership to support the student's ultimate success.

Sometimes helping means going beyond talking about school. If parents/caregivers don't understand the importance of supplying their tax returns on time, or have never done a tax return and are ashamed to ask for help, their child could be penalized in the allocation of financial aid. This mistake could hurt or even destroy her chances of going to college. It may seem strange to imagine a school where college counselors sit with adults and explain how a tax return works, but I work in such a school, and I notice that such work loses its sense of strangeness very quickly. I understand the argument that this is simply too much for a school to take on. But here is the equation, the raw truth: without this kind of work, stories like Shanita's and Ricardo's are going to continue. When we do the work, we reap the rewards. We see a young African American man begin his freshman year at the Berklee School of Music, knowing that he sent in his deposit. We see a young woman whose mother is in jail head off to BU. And we know that these things, despite the brilliance and hard work in the classroom, despite teachers like Ms. Sampson and advisors like Beth busting their butts, would not be possible without the extra step of working with families.

THE TRICKY ISSUE OF PARENT ACCESS TO POWER
IN THE SCHOOL: INVISIBLE BARRIERS ARE THERE
FOR ADULTS, TOO.

When BAA opened, the founding faculty was determined to honor
the contributions of parents. We wanted parents to understand and
buy in to our curriculum, our advising system, and our aspirations
for their children. We took seriously the importance of the parental role in their child's education, and we worked hard to create an
environment in which parents felt that they had a stake in their
student's success. We strove to make real the mantra so often heard
in educational circles and schools—"the importance of parental involvement." We expanded the term "parent" to include "caregiver"
because we knew that many of our students, like Ricardo, were not
being raised by biological parents. Our parent council was renamed
the Parent-Caregiver Council (PCC). However, we were not prepared for the historical patterns of race and class that so often prede-
termine who steps up to the plate of traditional parental involvement
in the parent council.

I know that many schools, maybe all schools, believe in parental
involvement. I hear my colleagues saying, "We *do* invite the parents
in. We even try to have interpreters for our non-English speaking
parents. But so much of the time they don't come anyway. So many
of my parents are working two and three jobs." Given how hard re-
cruiting parental involvement is, how can leaders do more than give
it lip service? In Boston, we now have a district-wide program called
"Technology Goes Home," which offers parents computer training
on Saturday mornings. After finishing training, they are eligible to
receive a computer. Perhaps we will find some answers to parental
involvement through the Internet. I'm excited about and supportive
of all these efforts. But I believe that the toughest nut to crack, and
one that principals regularly avoid because it makes us uncomfort-

able and vulnerable to backlash, is doing more than simply encouraging parents who typically do not serve as leaders to step up. We have to actually say the words—name the problem of race, specifically—to the parents themselves, just as we name it to the students.

Parents played a huge role in the opening of Boston Arts Academy and there was an expectation that the school would have a vibrant and dedicated Parent-Caregiver Council. The PCC, whose members were self-nominated, was clearly described in our early documents as being the representative body that would voice the concerns and ideas of all parents, and work with the faculty and administration to make sure that all students would receive an excellent education. Early in the PCC's history, its members advocated for BAA with politicians and city officials to guarantee that the school did not miss out on city funding. The council participated in strategic planning and elected representatives to the board of trustees, the school's governing board. And the PCC had been instrumental in garnering significant grants and recognition for the school.

Early on, I experienced a situation in which the parental involvement that I so touted threatened to compromise access; I was forced to deal with my own values and beliefs in a way that still makes me uncomfortable today. I tell this story because, when we seriously question and confront issues of access and equity, there is usually no script for how to proceed and no answer sheet with the correct response clearly delineated.

Sandra, one of BAA's founding parents, had been the leader in our first PCC. Sandra came from one of Boston's white neighborhoods and had been involved with city politics for years. She brought her enormous political acumen to the PCC and did a superb job getting city politicians into our school building so that they would know about and support our efforts. She managed to help pressure the city to finish the renovations on the building, and because of her connections, we were designated the "Mayor's School," a title that certainly held us in good stead whenever we needed to maneuver through byzantine Boston politics.

But the powerful, effective council Sandra created during our first few years was primarily populated with parents like herself who lived in white neighborhoods. There were a few African American parents and one Latina parent who attended when she could. Parents were involved in all aspects of the school under Sandra's leadership, but many of the conversations were skewed to the needs of the more middle-class students, and Ms. Torres and I were frustrated that our PCC never seemed to represent the range of students in terms of race and culture. The BAA parent coordinator, whose job it was to assist the PCC, was also disappointed at her inability, especially given that she was a woman of color, to address the racial imbalance of the PCC.

In our fourth year of operation, at our opening parent meeting, parents again self-nominated for elections. I looked at the array of parents who were running and I felt completely dismayed. Of the dozen or so volunteers, only one was a parent of color. I turned to our parent coordinator, Andrea Warren, and asked, "Should I say something? This just doesn't seem right."

She grimaced, and hesitated. Finally the words came out. "Well, we have passed out the ballots, but I guess you should. I'd hate to have another year where we regret the lack of diversity on the council when we could have done something about it."

I stood before the parents and began, "I hate to do this just before you are going to vote, but I have to ask us to look around the room and then look at who we have put forward for elections. I know each of the candidates is fantastic and wants to do the right thing for our school, but I also believe it is very important to have candidates who represent the diversity of our student body. You know, in 'the old days' during Judge Garrity's court orders for desegregation, we had to hold these elections by racial and ethnic groups. Starting in 1974, the Boston Public Schools required that parent councils reflected the racial makeup of the school community. African American parents elected their representatives, and white and Hispanic parents elected theirs. That's just the way we did it back then. We didn't always get nominations from every group so the councils weren't always representative even then, but we were required by law to be transparent about race. We haven't talked about that much here with our parent body." Then I recounted the demographics of our student body.

"I know we've closed nominations, but I feel that we need to really rethink that. Sometimes, as white people, we need to just wait and see what will happen if we don't step forward. If we don't, will someone else step forward? Maybe someone who hadn't considered running before? Maybe someone who doesn't look like me? Although we've had a very active parent council for four years, it has been predominantly white. Please don't interpret what I'm saying as a criticism of anyone, but in this school it doesn't seem right to have a predominantly white parent council. That just doesn't reflect our student body. It seems like we ought to be able to change that. We really need all of your voices and perspectives."

"Now, Linda…" Betty began. I'd known Betty for a long time. I had taught many of her children and nieces and nephews and godchildren. She is an African American woman who has always been deeply involved in the education of her children. "You can't mess with the process once things have closed. Nominations have finished. You needed to say your piece before. It's too late now." And she sat down. My cheeks burned with embarrassment. Of course Betty was right. In all the years I'd known her, she'd never publicly criticized me. I could feel the tension in the room and the anger of parents bubbling over.

Suddenly, Bob jumped up. "You know I'm sure it's illegal what you just did. This is a parent election. Principals can't influence the process like that. You have no right to say what you did. We could just take you to court or certainly report you to the superintendent.

This disgusts me. I know when I'm not wanted. You can take my slot and give it to someone you want to have on the council. That way you won't even have to have nominations. Go ahead and just appoint someone who's not white since that's obviously what you are going to do anyway. So much for elections and fair processes and all." Bob stormed out of the room. A number of the white parents got up and left with him. Mickie stayed. I caught her eye and she looked down. One of her children had graduated the year before, and she was one of the strongest supporters of the school. She was on the council. Bob was also her friend. I could tell she didn't want to be associated with me at that moment.

I turned to the parent coordinator to see if she would intervene. A woman of color, she appeared just as uncomfortable as I was at this moment. None of us seemed to know what to do.

After what seemed to be an interminable moment, Pamela, an African American parent new to the school, spoke up. "I've been involved in a lot of parent councils before. Usually I'm the only parent of color. I didn't run tonight because I'm a new parent and I wanted a year to get to know the school. Also, I assumed that since the students are over 75 percent students of color, parents of color would be more involved in the council. I have seen over the years that it is always hard for us. We don't have the traditions of running for office in this country. We don't have it on school councils either. We are often on the outside looking in. I did think it would be different here. I know the process tonight has been bad, but I would like to suggest we open up nominations one more time. Maybe now that we've said out loud that we want more parents of color to run, more of us will. If we do open up nominations, I will put myself forward."

Betty struggled back to her feet. To my surprise she said, "I move that we open up nominations again." One of the white parents standing up who had self-nominated seconded the motion. He sat down.

"Okay," the parent coordinator began, "let's just start again. Who wants to nominate themselves?"

Mickie stood up. "I've been on the council for three years. I think I've done a good job and I've gotten a lot of things for the school. Ms. Nathan always calls me because I have a lot of connections. But I'm not going to run. Maybe Ms. Nathan doesn't think I have much to contribute anymore. So I will take back my nomination." She sat down. I felt terrible. Bob had left. Mickie was clearly angry. How could I have done this differently? As my thoughts and self-criticism raced, Pamela nominated herself. So did Betty. So did four other African American women. Suddenly the pool of nominees looked very different than it had before.

As the nominees introduced themselves, I stood near Mickie. She clearly wanted no discussion or contact with me, but I felt that if I just stood near her, she might feel that I still really respected and appreciated her work on behalf of the school. In that awful moment, this small gesture was all I could think of to do.

The elections were held. The results gave us a council in which 70 percent of the members were parents of color. A few more announcements closed out the meeting and then I spoke before wishing everyone good night: "I am really sorry about my process tonight. I know that I infuriated many of you, but I'm also pleased at the results of the election. It is so important with the work we are doing with our students that they see parents of color involved with the school and in positions of leadership. I don't mean to devalue anyone's contributions and we will work to keep everyone involved. I appreciate you staying tonight."

Bob sent an angry e-mail to the PCC stating that what I had done was illegal and that he was considering suing the school. He said the elections should be nullified, and we should all come back together and start again, without me in the room. He didn't get much response from other members of the council. An African American parent thanked me for speaking out but suggested that, in the future, I get other parents to deliver the message so that there wouldn't be such anger directed at me.

I ask myself whether it would have been better for a parent to deliver the message that I had given so clumsily and with such bad timing. I don't think so. I think it's important that I, as an authority figure, intervened when things were going badly. I couldn't face "keeping the secret" of another year with a nearly all-white council. Do we not act because we are afraid of angering or embarrassing parents? Or, is it because we are actually embarrassed and afraid? My actions, which seemed insensitive and perhaps illegal to some parents, changed the course of events for our Parent-Caregiver Council elections. Since that year, we have had a very diverse council. We have also talked about that disruptive election. I begin each council meeting acknowledging the importance of our diversity and how we have worked hard to achieve it. I think it's vital that parents know our history so that we don't fall backward again. One year a parent even asked, "Is diversity a problem here?" She was looking at a Parent-Caregiver Council that was mixed by race and even gender.

An African American parent, the cochair, answered. "Well, given that BAA is a microcosm of the larger U.S., I'd say issues of race, class, and gender are always difficult and require continual attention." This parent continued, "Are we truly mixed by social class? What about parents of students with special needs? Where are our parents who don't speak English as their first language? Yeah, I'd say diversity is a problem and we'd better keep working at it."

There were nods around the table. Vanessa, an African American mom, said, "We need to always listen to our kids. They talk about the mix of students in this school. They talk about the challenges, too. What they like and what they don't like. But they know there is more discussion about diversity here than anywhere else."

Mickie sat at the table, too. "You know I'm not on the council this year either. I was, in the first years. But now I'm on the Political Action Committee. You know why I'm not on the council?" She looked directly at me. I thought about that meeting a few years back. "I heard you a few years ago. When you talked about letting others step forward, I was angry with you. I thought you didn't care about what I could bring to the school. I took back my nomination. I really hated that you created such a charged situation. So much about Boston is about race. Most of us who grew up here are products of desegregation. It's part of our past. It's painful. It's embarrassing. I went to South Boston during the riots. I still live there, but I always treat everyone as an individual. When you talked to us like that a few years ago, you didn't see us as individuals. It was just like during busing. We were just racial groups. You made it seem like we had nothing to contribute. But I'm still here. I have found other ways to participate. "

I wanted to hug Mickie. She hadn't liked what I said, or when I had said it, but her present actions spoke louder than her past reactions. She had stepped down. She hadn't run for council then or now. But rather than backing away, she had remained involved in the school. She was, in fact, leading our Political Action Committee. She helped organize a teacher appreciation event. She came to council meetings and board meetings, but she didn't vote. She made sure that other parents, who didn't look like her, or come from her background, were on the council. She understood the complexity of exhibiting allied behavior—of white people putting themselves in other positions in order to support people of color taking charge.

As a white leader, I had felt compelled to say what I did that year in order to change the landscape of our council. Providing access doesn't always mean going with the status quo, and making changes can be very threatening, complicated, and hard. Making mistakes can also be a productive learning experience. At that PCC election, I felt I had to silence some groups in order for others to emerge. For me, that was access.

I wanted to be a principal who listened to everyone and provided equal access for everyone. But this clearly wasn't working at our PCC elections. Should I have just stood by and wished that things had turned out differently? Or, as in our work as a faculty, did I have an obligation to present the data and be open about the problems? To be explicit about what was happening right here regarding access? My cheeks still burn with embarrassment when I think about my lousy timing and lousy process. But the diversity and strength of our council today is well worth the pain of that memory. Last year, after many years with few or no Latino representatives on the council, we had our first Latino cochair. All parents, from every background, celebrated this important accomplishment.

WHERE DO WE GO FROM HERE?

Success in the current educational structure seems to be based on a mythology of miracles. Story after story is told about the visionary teacher, counselor, or administrator who did so much for an individual student or class against terrible odds. The accepted wisdom has become that to be a good teacher, counselor, or administrator you must be a miracle worker. You must personally take a student from poverty and into the middle class.

I disagree. Our experiences at BAA have taught us that our work in urban education is much more complex than any one simple act of goodness or miracle making for one particular student. We honor all our students' backgrounds while offering them the skills to access opportunities that are very different from the ones they have known. Too many young people who grow up in oppressive conditions of poverty and poor schooling discount the possibilities of trying to "make it." We hear young people talk calmly and realistically about their chances of being dead before they reach the age of twenty-one, or about the "fact" that education doesn't guarantee a good job anyway, or that no matter how hard one tries, hardship is the only reward. Our kids have learned these "facts" from their parents, from their surroundings, and from their life experiences. Our job as teachers is to try to convince our kids that seemingly inaccessible opportunities and social goods are, with hard work and preparation, theirs for the taking. We want to give them an alternate set of facts—the real ones.

Our students are fully aware of the current codes of power—about who "makes it in school" or who gets the "good jobs" or into the "good colleges." The solution to increasing access in our schools is not to blame kids, teachers, or parents. It is not about blaming poverty, violence, or race. It is not about layering on more standardized tests. It is about figuring out how to talk about race, class, gender, language, and culture in classrooms, within the entire school and in our broader communities. It is about understanding that solutions must involve new processes, practices, and structures that will break those codes of power that define class and race privilege and have historically undermined so many of our students and denied them access. These solutions involve explicitly teaching about available opportunities, including the skills required to access available opportunities and to create new ones.

Just when we think that we have addressed all the possible questions about access, there will be another one that confounds us. We must be vigilant about learning our students' and parents' cultural histories. We must understand, deeply, who they are, where they come from, what their family arrangements look like, and how familiar their family may or may not be with the college admissions process and with the codes of power. At BAA we have realized through our failures with Shanita, Ricardo, and many others that access alone is not enough. On the surface, both Shanita and Ricardo had access to opportunities. They had earned the grades and had the accomplishments to merit acceptance at prestigious colleges, but we, as their teachers and administrators, had not completely understood the obstacles they face.

BAA cannot ever afford to say, "We get it! Now we understand how to provide access and to combat racism and classism." However, we can say that we know more now than we did ten years ago about the minefields our students will encounter. We are more conscious and steadily committed to helping our students avoid the traps they can fall into through our failure to recognize the invisible barriers they face.

We are pleased that 95 percent of our students attend college. Many more are attending four-year colleges than when we began. We are pleased that more are staying in college to earn their degrees than in our early years. This is all good news, but it is not enough. Too many of our students leave college for financial reasons, and too many attend colleges so close to their home environments that they cannot fully immerse themselves in the collegiate environment.

The idea that education is about liberation, as Freire wrote in the early 1960s, still eludes too many of our students. The promise that rang around the world at that time was that the power of the word, of reading, could change one's world. That is our intention at BAA. Books are our weapons. We put them into the hands of our young artist-scholars in as many different ways and forms as we can. We work around the clock to convince our young people that finishing high school and going on to college or a professional career is the ticket to freedom and a fulfilled life. We also present our students with the current statistics showing that holders of bachelor's degrees earn 70 percent more than those with just a high school diploma. Freedom is about making informed choices, creating one's own destiny, being an agent of change, or having agency, the ability to make decisions about one's own life. That is why we strive to make access like a piece of clothing, or a cloak, that all our students can put on with ease and comfort. Our students are learning how to break down the walls that have stood in their way for too long.

We know that education has become a key sorter of Americans into educational haves and have-nots. We see the inequities that our students face on a daily basis. It is our responsibility to ensure that our students can make visible those invisible threads of access. This enormous job requires that we have difficult, embarrassing, and angry conversations, as I did with the PCC. It requires working far beyond the confines of the school walls and the school day, and accepting that as urban educators, this is part of our job whether we want it to be or not. If we believe, as we do, that liberation *is* possible for our students, and that liberation is synonymous with access to and preparation for higher education, then the work before us is quite clear: an open door is not enough. If we are to change the status quo, rage must be our companion, and we must insist, through our actions as well as our words, that Shanita and Ricardo belong in the world of opportunity in every possible way.

Conclusion

The tenth-grade humanities class at BAA was finishing a unit on immigration. They had read excerpts of memoirs in which immigrants described the identity conflicts that arose from arriving in a new country. Students had explored their own immigrant heritage, and today's activity was to create a piece of art through printmaking that captured aspects of the student's own identity.

Haydee peeled her print off the small printing press and her expectant smile collapsed into a frown. "Ugh!" she cried. "It's just a blob! It's sooooo ugly." She threw it onto the drying table.

Her humanities teacher gently approached her. "Let me take a look, Haydee."

"It's too stupid. It's not at all about my identity. You can't even see the Puerto Rican flag, and you can't tell those are music notes at all. Just give me an F. I've never been any good at art. I'm a musician." Haydee stomped away and sat by herself.

Ms. Marsh, head of visual arts, happened to be in the room during this interaction and went up to Haydee. "Would you show me your print?" Haydee began the same explanation by pointing out how the musical notes were now a blob of blue instead of a clear, crisp outline. The inside of the Puerto Rican flag had spread into an oozing rectangle and the two hearts that framed the print also had swelled. The lines were not clean as Haydee had wanted.

"You're a musician, right?" Ms. Marsh asked, rhetorically, since she had known Haydee since her freshman year. "You learn to play the precise notes in tune with your ensemble or in big band. If you make a mistake it's heard immediately and then the music is jarring." Haydee nodded in agreement.

Ms. Marsh went on. "Printmaking also has precision and a defined technique, but art can have other purposes, too. Sometimes the intention or expectation we bring to a piece disappoints us. You wanted clean lines and you're mad that you didn't get them. But what we learn in visual arts is that sometimes we need to let the process take us to another place."

Ms. Marsh took hold of Haydee's arm at her wrist. "We start here," Ms. Marsh said, firming placing Haydee's arm in a space in the air. "And then we end here." Ms. Marsh guided Haydee's arm in a wide arc. Haydee's eyes followed the path her arm had made. "It's a place we didn't plan to be, and a place we may not even understand yet."

"Look at these notes," Ms. Marsh returned her attention to the actual print. "I see a shadow here, not a blob. I want to know what that shadow might represent for you."

Before Ms. Marsh could say another sentence, Haydee interrupted her. "Oooh, see the flag. See how it's smeared. Yeah, I didn't want it like that, but it's about my identity, and I'm not living in Puerto Rico anymore. I'm spread across two places—on the island and here in Boston."

"Exactly," Ms. Marsh said. "That's what I mean by allowing the process to take you to another place. So how could you draw on the print to extend that idea? What could you do with the notes?"

Haydee began to brainstorm ways that she could use a black pen to outline the shadow and even make it three-dimensional. As she shared her emerging ideas, another classmate approached her and said, "I love your print. I really like the way everything runs together." Haydee smiled at Ms. Marsh.

o   o   o

This small journey between a teacher and a student happens many times a day at BAA in both arts and academic classes. The results are not always positive. Sometimes students storm off, and the teacher is unable, in the moment, to lure them back into a positive, engaged demeanor. But, more often than not, the teacher is able to redirect a student and help them to find a way through a problem or a disappointment into a place of emerging success.

Other times, even with all the work teachers do, students are still derailed. They make the wrong choices. They lack the judgment that we educators think we are teaching them to have. Unfortunately, these cases are not as exceptional as I wish they were, but as they bring us up short, they also remind us of the conditions against which we—students and faculty—labor, and how those conditions can prove too much for us to overcome.

After Ricardo graduated, even though he had missed all the financial aid deadlines, he was still determined to attend college. He dreamed of becoming an architect. He had worked for a year in a design firm doing gopher jobs, and then returned to Ms. Hairston for help with college financial aid applications. He was admitted to a two-year college with financial aid and was both working and attending school. The faculty was proud of him. His advisor stayed in close touch with him and he had been checking in about his progress often. Ricardo had done well in his drafting class, but he was struggling with his attendance since he needed to work so many hours.

I was surprised when his grandmother called BAA for help. "I didn't know who else to call," she said to me through tears. "You all were his family. I don't know why he did this." She told me that her grandson had been arrested with a loaded weapon. Although he had not shot the gun, he was now in jail. "He was going to college. Why did he need to go and do that? I told him about running the streets with those friends of his. I told him if he didn't just stick to class and work he'd end up like them. They are no good. But he never did listen to me."

I didn't know what to say. All that came out of my mouth was, "I'm just so sorry. I'm so sorry." I wanted to cry on the other end of the phone. How could this be possible? Ricardo had so much potential and had struggled profoundly to keep his "eyes on the prize." What had gone wrong? So many of us at BAA had been advocating for him. I asked if I could call his lawyer. Perhaps if I wrote a letter about his character and my sense of his potential that would help his case.

"I would appreciate that." His grandmother sighed. "I'm just tired," she went on. "My health isn't good. I may not even be able to make it to the court date. But a letter from you all . . ." Her voiced was choked. "Maybe because he was good there that will help the case." I also asked if I could visit him in jail. His grandmother put me on the list of visitors.

Ricardo's lawyer agreed that a letter from me on our letterhead and also from Mr. McCaffery, head of Student Support, would help. Since Ricardo had no previous convictions, perhaps he would not face too serious a punishment. I wondered about his financial aid and about whether he would ever finish college.

My brief visit with him in jail left me despondent. The usual brightness in his eyes was gone. He seemed years older. His shoulders drooped and he didn't have much to say. "Why?" was about the only question I could ask. "I don't know," was his answer. "I just wasn't thinking." I could feel his shame. He didn't really seem to want me there. I tried to make small talk. "Has your grandmother been able to come see you?"

"No. She isn't feeling very strong," Ricardo answered.

I told him about seeing some of his high school friends at BAA the other week. "Yeah, I heard Mike was doing real well," he commented wistfully.

"We are all pulling for you," I finally assured him. "I've written a strong letter about your character. So has Mr. McCaffery. Maybe that will help reduce your sentence."

"Thank you for doing that. I know it sounds lame, but if I could go back in time and change everything I would. At the arts academy I was somebody and now that's been ruined. I know how much everyone there helped me."

"Mr. McCaffery will try and be at your court date. I've asked your grandmother to let us know when it is." Ricardo nodded his thanks. There seemed like nothing more to say.

The judge was lenient with Ricardo. He was let out on bail and put on probation, but he was a changed person—much more hardened and cynical. He had, of course, missed too many classes to return to college that semester. Mr. McCaffery called him and reminded him that he could still return to college. Ricardo said he had bills to pay and needed to be working. He owed his grandmother and others the bail money. He has still not returned to college. He doesn't return Mr. McCaffery's calls anymore. He seems to have decided to slip away.

The arts didn't hold Ricardo. Neither could we, his teachers and advocates. Still, Ricardo's actions don't change how much we still care about him and want the best for him. Even though I sense that Ricardo has given up hope of ever really pursuing a career, I haven't. Neither has Mr. McCaffery or Ms. Hairston. We can't stop hoping to see him again, to connect again, to help Ricardo find a way to return to college. Sometimes we feel like Sisyphus, continually pushing the rocks back up the mountain as quickly as they fall down, nearly crushing us. But we cannot afford to languish in dismal and hopeless metaphors. Our students matter to us—each one deeply and personally—and we cannot see them as throwaways like so much of society would have us do. That is why we are determined to keep trying—no matter what. We say to one another, "While just one of us has breath and strength left, we won't forsake our kids." While that may sound like missionary zeal, we know we can't "save the children." We openly and honestly acknowledge that we may not succeed, but we *will* keep at the work.

I have argued for a robust arts education to be included in all schools. More broadly, I would argue that successful schools need to stand for something that everyone in the school community can identify, describe, and subscribe to. I can imagine many different approaches—sciences, health, physical fitness, social justice, or a combination of all or some of these. Our students are waiting for us, the adults, to take the lead. These young people know that the schools they currently inhabit are not as good as they should be. They want to belong, to feel empowered, to express their passions, but too many of them are not living in environments that invite them to do so.

BAA's solid foundation in the arts has given all of us permission to reimagine our school continually, despite the many constraints that surround us. Difficult questions about school structure; teacher-student relationships; curriculum; assessment; family involvement; issues of race, class, language, and culture; and the role of a professional learning community—all have been in the forefront of our decade-long evolution. And the language of the arts has given us a constructive way to describe our ideas and practices.

I hope that our stories from BAA will give other educators the opportunity to debate and question their own successes and stumbling blocks. If I've learned anything during my years in schools it is that change can only come from a rigorous questioning process. And as it's often said: "Change is hard, you go first." I hope to provoke and inspire the reader to pose new questions.

I am frustrated by how little the public really understands about what urban schools need. Why isn't there an uproar or revolt at the ways in which our schools are currently structured or at the constraints that are being imposed on teachers and principals, whether it be through school districts or union policies? The notion that this country can carry on blindly with test after test as if children's futures aren't being wasted strikes me as being completely insane. As educators, we cannot be expected on our own to stem the tide of rising violence in our cities; we can, however, and we must, demand opportunities to use the time we do have with students in our school buildings to address those issues.

I believe that, despite all the ills that currently infect our schools, we, the practitioners, can prevail over current misguided policies that impede possibilities for improved student achievement. Even though there is much wrong with schools in our country, we must hold tenaciously to those moments that reflect larger possibilities. Without continual opportunities to rethink and to pose questions and search for answers to some of the most intractable problems in our schools, educators will not be able to productively and thoughtfully engage in the most important of debates: that of how to narrow the achievement gap.

And I believe that the telling of one school's story will open some doors on recommendations for new policy development. I am pleased that at BAA we have not allowed the constraints to stop the journey. Granted, we have benefited from larger freedoms because of our pilot school status, but my hope is that our story will inspire other educators to demand similar conditions under which to operate.

I offer the following recommendations to all educators and policy makers in the hopes that they might constitute the beginning of a long and undeniably arduous conversation:

- o Develop a clear strategy, for students, parents, and teachers, of active engagement and ownership of the educational process.

○   Investigate the possibilities of incorporating, for example, an arts-based, science-based, or technology-based curriculum into every high school.

○   Require a rigorous Senior Project that successfully reflects academic and non-academic learning as well as addressing a community need, recognized and documented by the student.

○   Build an assessment system that doesn't determine student achievement and knowledge exclusively through the results of standardized tests.

○   Mandate paid time for teachers to talk about their practice and their students, and struggle with the difficult questions.

○   Advocate for our public schools to equalize educational facilities, expand curricular opportunities, and reduce class size to match our best schools, thus providing every child with the necessary education and skills to participate productively in our democracy. This necessarily costs more money!

At BAA, the faculty has worked at all of these, but I have no doubt that my readers will come up with recommendations of their own.

We are enormously proud of our students' abilities to negotiate across barriers of race, culture, and class, as well as their skills of empathy and knowing how to do the right thing. We want all our students to have good test scores; we want them to succeed in college and their careers; but more than anything we want them to understand what it means to give to a larger community. And they do: our students are acting in local theater productions, dancing with emerging companies, working in various industries, and going on to graduate schools. We see them as mentors and role models in arts organizations across the city. They are the next generation of arts educators; the next generation of teachers; and the next generation of young people who will make sure to always ask the hard questions.

The students are successful in large part because of the resilience of their teachers at BAA who continue to put in the time and effort to direct and redirect them even when students misstep again and again. When violence claims the life of a student, as happened recently, or when one of them ends up in jail because of poor choices, our work seems insurmountable and impossible.

Faculty members find strength in one another and their school community. Teachers embrace; they hold each other tightly as a student's tragedy unfolds. They keep telling one another that their students will pull through and that even when situations like Ricardo's happen, teachers cannot be defeated. They may *feel* defeated, but they cannot *be* defeated. There is a big difference. They keep producing their own work—as artist-scholars. They keep persevering.

It is this untold valor of the BAA community that I celebrate here. Slowly the rest of the educational world is also coming to recognize the positive innovations of our faculty and learn from them. Our teachers have won awards for excellence in teaching and guidance, and numerous objective research studies focused on our school all describe the work of this dedicated faculty.

It takes great courage to persist in seeking success in the face of lack of funding, tests that limit curriculum and do not adequately reflect student achievement, little or no professional time, and a lamentable disconnect between policy makers and practitioners. I have written this book to tell the story of that courage, of how at BAA we have explored and discovered new shadows and shapes where others might have settled for seeing only an indeterminate blob of color. A Boston Arts Academy alumnus, and Brown University graduate, recently said to me, "I am proof that a BAA education works. We've just got to keep telling people that." And so, I am.

Acknowledgments

In my first classroom I taped on the wall a favorite stanza of a poem by the Spanish poet, Antonio Machado. It reminded me daily why I entered the teaching profession.

> Caminante,
> No hay camino
> Se hace el camino al andar

My clunky translation is:

> Traveler,
> There is no path
> We make the path by walking

It is that last line that has always captured my imagination. It could be translated as "one" makes the path in a particularly individual way. Or "we" make our path together. Both interpretations work for me.

I wasn't sure that I would be able to stay on this writing path and finish this book, but I have been fortunate to have extraordinary encouragement and collaboration as I have journeyed. My husband, Steven

Cohen, has provided daily support and love even when I exasperated him! You are the best teacher I know. My parents, Jean and David, were terrific cheerleaders. They reminded me to keep my sense of humor and they gave me valuable advice every step of the way.

Thank you to the many who worked with me—formally and informally as editors, readers, advisors, and writing coaches: Abdi Ali, Anne Clark, Sam Cohen, Steve Cohen, Jill Davidson, Jessica Davis, Susan Heath, Swanee Hunt, Andy Hyrcyna, Jill Kneerim, Samara Lopez, Hilary Maddox, Sarah Mayper, Deborah Meier, Ed Miller, Ann Moritz, Christine Renaud, Alexis Rizzuto, Carole Salz, Eileen Shakespear, Ted and Nancy Sizer, Susan Werbe.

This book is born from the belief that Vito first had: that I could, in fact, capture experiences and stories that others would want to read. If it hadn't been for Vito I would have never met Debbie and Ann Cook and the many others who have been so instrumental in my work.

To my best friend, Janie Ward, who listened to every writing woe and then came up with solutions, thank you for your guidance, your firm hand, and your love. I couldn't have done this without you.

"If we don't tell our own stories, someone else will," a wise friend told me. I hope that those teachers, principals, and parents with whom I have had the honor to work will catch a glimpse of themselves, their ideas, and their stories here.

o   o   o

And to the best "co's" anyone could hope for...thank you Larry Myatt and Carmen Torres for the friendship and the fun.

Abigail Boone Schirmer was one of the most inspiring teachers I have ever worked with. She always understood that the hardest questions were the most important ones.

Amy Waldman believed in this book long before I did. I wish she could read it.

The Boston Arts Academy Board of Trustees and the Boston Arts Academy Foundation have also invested in me and the school in countless ways. Thank you to each and every one of you who has given so generously of your time, talent, treasure, and wisdom. This school is every bit a reflection of your core values and passions.

Thank you to the entire BAA founding faculty, the Fenway teachers who taught me so much, and all the current BAA faculty, parents, and students. Many of you are reflected in these pages and many of you have read numerous drafts. In some cases I have used your actual names; in many cases I have obscured individual identities. I hope I have represented all of you respectfully.